# CLINICAL PSYCHOPHARMACOLOGY

**made
ridiculously
simple**

Bret A. Moore, Psy.D., ABPP
*Independent Practice*
*San Antonio, Texas*

John Preston, Psy.D., ABPP
*Alliant International University*
*Sacramento, California*

James Johnson, M.D.
*Kaiser Medical Center*
*Department of Psychiatry*
*South Sacramento, California*

**MEDMASTER**

ISBN 13# 978-1-935660-40-8

*Made in the United States of America*

Cover Illustrations by Jordan Collver

Published by
MedMaster, Inc.
P.O. Box 640028
Miami, Fla. 33164

*For Cindy Lolo (JP)*
*For  Lori, Kaitlyn, Chester, Charity & Duchess (BAM)*

# Contents

# Preface

This brief book provides an overview of clinical psychopharmacology. Successful medical treatment of emotional and mental disorders depends on two factors: a thorough knowledge of psychotropic medications and an accurate diagnosis. Both issues are addressed in this book in a practical and concise format.

To the best of our knowledge, recommended doses for medications listed in this book are accurate. However, they are not meant to serve as a guide for prescription of medications. Please check the manufacturer's product information sheet or the *Physicians' Desk Reference* for any changes in dosage schedule or contraindications.

We wish to express our appreciation to the following people who have reviewed this book and made a number of helpful suggestions: John H. Greist, M.D., Donald Klein, M.D., Glen Hakanson, M.D., and Patrick Donlon, M.D. Many thanks to Michelle Riekstins for her help in the preparation of the manuscript and to our editor, Dr. Stephen Goldberg, for many helpful suggestions.

# Chapter 1    General Principles

## BIOLOGY vs. PSYCHOLOGY

For many years a debate raged in psychiatry with regard to the etiology and treatment of major mental disorders. Two opposing camps emerged: biological psychiatry, whose devotees held that psychiatric disorders had an organic basis; and psychologically oriented psychiatry, probably best represented by the psychodynamic movement, whose converts focused on the role of current emotional stressors, early childhood traumas, interpersonal problems, and intrapsychic conflict as causal agents in the development of psychiatric symptomatology. Although these polar views still exist, in recent years there has been an emerging view that encompasses both psychological and physiological factors in the etiology and treatment of many psychiatric disorders. In many, if not most, mental disorders it is helpful to think of a continuum or spectrum. Almost all mental disorders usually represent heterogeneous syndromes.

When one talks about depression, for instance, it is important to realize that depression can present in a number of different ways and may have diverse etiologies. In some instances the cause may be purely psychological, e.g., a reaction to losing a job, death of a loved one, a significant rejection, etc. Likewise, symptoms may be largely psychological, e.g., feelings of low self-esteem and sadness. In other cases the picture is one of a pure biological disorder which has little or no connection to environmental precipitants, but rather involves an endogenous neurochemical malfunction. In addition to psychological symptoms, the resulting symptoms may include a host of somatic symptoms, such as sleep disturbance and weight loss. Clearly, in some individuals there is an interplay of environmental/psychological factors *and* biochemical dysfunctions. The question "Is this a psychological or biological problem?" is overly simplistic. Rather, one must ask, "To what extent is this disorder due to psychological factors and to what extent is it due to a biochemical disturbance?" The answer to this question is extremely important in guiding treatment decisions. *Most purely psychological problems are not helped by medication treatment. On the other hand, most biologically based psychiatric disorders require medication treatment.*

In this book we hope to provide key diagnostic guidelines to help the clinician pinpoint the diagnosis and develop a realistic treatment plan.

## PHARMACOLOGY

Pharmacology is the science of how drugs work in the body, and by extension, psychopharmacology is the science of how drugs work in the brain and affect our thoughts, feelings, and behavior. Although it is not necessary to understand pharmacology in great detail, having basic familiarity with a few concepts lays the groundwork for the chapters that follow. The two most important pharmacological principles to be aware of are pharmacodynamics and pharmacokinetics.

*Pharmacodynamics* is simply defined as what the drug does to the body. As a drug is introduced to and circulates throughout a person's system, it attaches to receptors on cells in the brain and body. Ideally, this connection between the medication and receptors in the brain will lead to a therapeutic response (i.e. less depression or anxiety). How a specific person responds is influenced by a variety of factors to include the dose of the medication, the type of receptor(s) targeted by the drug, and the presence of other drugs. Pharmacodynamics also explains how and why people experience drug side effects. For example, the antidepressant fluoxetine (Prozac) is effective for depression and anxiety because it attaches to receptors in the brain that are fond of the chemical serotonin. Serotonin regulates mood and anxiety. However, the vast majority of serotonin receptors reside in the gut. Since serotonin attaches to receptors throughout the entire body and not just the brain, medications like fluoxetine commonly lead to the side effects of nausea, diarrhea, and constipation.

Conversely, *pharmacokinetics* is defined as what the body does to the drug. There are four primary processes to understand: absorption, distribution, metabolism, and elimination. Absorption is the movement of the drug from the site of administration to the bloodstream. In other words, after taking a medication how does the drug enter the system so it can start to do its job. The rate of absorption is determined by the route of administration. Oral administration (i.e. taking a pill) is the slowest because the pill must make its way through the stomach and intestines before it hits the bloodstream. Intravenous (i.e. injecting the drug directly into the vein) is the fastest as the medication immediately enters the bloodstream. Distribution is the movement of the drug in the bloodstream to receptors within the brain and body. The level of distribution is dependent on body composition (e.g. proportion of fat versus muscle) and disease states like kidney or cardiovascular disease. Metabolism is the process that prepares the medication to be eliminated from the body. As the medication circulates throughout the system, it passes through the liver. One of the main functions of the liver is to break down drugs so they can be excreted. The last process is elimination. The elimination of drugs occurs primarily through the kidneys. The chemical structure of the drug and kidney health of the person determines how rapidly and efficiently the drug is removed from the system.

# Chapter 2    Depression

## DIAGNOSIS

### Major Clinical Features and Differential Diagnosis

It is important to distinguish between (1) reactive sadness, (2) grief, (3) medical illness and medications that cause depressive symptoms, (4) clinical depression (also commonly referred to as unipolar or major depression), and (5) dysthymia. The first two are painful but normal emotional reactions and usually do not require medical treatment. These five syndromes may be distinguished by the following characteristics:

1. *Reactive Sadness.* The emotional reaction stems from a relatively minor event. It is transient (a few hours to a few days) and rarely interferes with functioning.

2. *Grief.* This is a normal response to a major interpersonal loss (such as the death of a loved one or marital separation/divorce). This experience can be tremendously painful and is much more prolonged than reactive sadness. Please note that "normal" grief can last for many months and it is not uncommon for noticeable sadness and loneliness to persist for several years following significant interpersonal losses. Grief differs from clinical depression in four ways:

   a. Despite intense sadness, there is no significant loss of self-esteem.

   b. Markers that grief has developed into clinical depression include: severe sleep disturbances (especially early morning awakening), a pervasive loss of interest in normal life activities, significant agitation, and/or suicidal ideations.

   c. The patient clearly relates the sadness to the loss. There may be active mourning and pining for the loved one; the painful feelings "make sense."

   d. Grief work (i.e., mourning) and time are often the major ingredients necessary for emotional healing.

   Note that at least 25% of people experiencing a major loss will initially exhibit grief reactions, but during the year following the loss will go on to develop major depression (Persistent Complex Bereavement Disorder: DSM-5, 2013). Additionally, 10% of bereaved individuals will develop traumatic stress symptoms following interpersonal losses (e.g.. intense anxiety, nightmares). Thus one must have a high index of suspicion for these common forms of complicated bereavement.

3. *Medical Illnesses and Medications That Can Cause Depression.* Certain medical disorders (see Figure 1) can at times result in biochemical changes

that affect central neurotransmitters, thereby triggering serious depressive reactions. Hypothyroidism (especially subclinical presentations) is clearly the most common medical disorder causing depressive symptoms (accounting for 5-10% of major depressions), thus it is always important to screen for thyroid disease. Likewise, some medications can cause depression as a side effect (see Figure 2). Please note that minor tranquilizers may cause or exacerbate depression. A very frequent treatment mistake is for the physician to be impressed by the more obvious symptoms of anxiety or agitation, to fail to recognize an underlying depression, and to only prescribe a benzodiazepine/minor tranquilizer. (Note: 50% of cases of major depression are accompanied by significant anxiety or agitation.) The result is often some initial calming, but after a few weeks the depression worsens. If the basic disorder is depression, but with coexisting anxiety symptoms, it is important to treat the depression. With appropriate treatment for the depression, the anxiety symptoms will generally subside.

It is very important to note that it is common during periods of depression for patients to significantly increase their use of caffeine. Caffeine of course combats fatigue, but it also has mild, transient antidepressant actions, and thus people gravitate towards increasing use. This results in a commonly overlooked complication to treatment: caffeine amounts in excess of 250 mg. per day can contribute to a decrease in slow wave (deep) sleep; slow wave sleep is already decreased in depression and the further erosion of this form of restorative sleep often worsens depression. Caffeine also contributes to restless sleep and frequent awakenings during the night. It is important for patients to know that this effect can occur even in the absence of initial insomnia. This is such a pervasive problem that it is essential to take a caffeine history on *all* patients suffering from psychiatric disorders (please see Appendix C for a brief caffeine questionnaire). With depression every attempt should be made to keep caffeine consumption below 250 mg a day (and preferably used only in the morning). Many patients will not take such recommendations seriously unless the health care professional makes a point to explain its impact on sleep.

When the basic cause of depression is one of the illnesses listed in Figure 1 or a side effect of medication, the primary focus should be on treating the core illness or switching medications. When such interventions are carried out, the depression will usually lift.

4. *Clinical Depression.* This is a pathological process characterized as follows:

   a. Depressed mood (sadness or emptiness) or irritability is often continuous and pervasive.

   b. A loss of interest in normal life activities.

   c. There is increasing impairment of normal functioning (work, school, and intimate relationships).

   d. There is an irrational or exaggerated erosion of self-esteem.

## Figure 1

### COMMON DISORDERS THAT MAY CAUSE DEPRESSION

- Addison's disease
- AIDS
- Alzheimer's disease
- Anemia
- Apnea
- Asthma
- Chronic Fatigue Syndromes
- Chronic infection (mononucleosis, TB)
- Chronic pain
- Congestive heart failure
- Cushing's disease
- Diabetes
- Hyperthyroidism
- Hypothyroidism
- Infectious Hepatitis
- Influenza
- Lyme disease
- Malignancies (cancer)
- Malnutrition
- Menopause
- Multiple sclerosis
- Parkinson's disease
- Post-partum hormonal changes
- Porphyria
- Premenstrual syndrome
- Restless legs
- Rheumatoid arthritis
- Sleep apnea
- Syphilis
- Systemic lupus erythematosis
- Ulcerative colitis
- Uremia

   e. There is a dramatic and specific change in vegetative patterns (e.g., sleep, appetite, sex drive, etc.) and the appearance of nonspecific physical complaints.

   f. Depression can occur in response to psychological stressors, or may emerge without clear-cut precipitating events.

5. *Dysthymia* (also called *Persistent Depressive Disorder*): low-grade, chronic depression. Long-standing dysphoria, irritability, low-self-esteem and often a lack of enthusiasm. This condition is less severe than clinical depression and typically does not interfere with daily functioning.

## Target Symptoms

All types of depression tend to share certain universal symptoms (see Figure 3). Disorders that reflect an underlying biochemical dysfunction typically present with *both* the universal symptoms *and* the physiological symptoms (Figure 4).

## ANTIDEPRESSANT MEDICATION

## When Do You Prescribe Antidepressants?

The most important guideline for prescribing antidepressant medication is whether or not there are sustained physiological symptoms, as outlined below (see Figure 4). Occasional disturbances of sleep or appetite, for instance, do not warrant

*Figure 2*

## DRUGS THAT MAY CAUSE DEPRESSION

| TYPE | GENERIC NAME | BRAND NAME |
|------|-------------|-----------|
| ■ *Antihypertensives* (for high blood pressure) | reserpine | Serpasil, Ser-Ap-Es, Sandril |
| | propranolol hydrochloride | Inderal |
| | methyldopa | Aldomet |
| | guanethidine sulfate | Ismelin sulfate |
| | clonidine hydrochloride | Catapres |
| | hydralazine hydrochloride | Apresoline hydrochloride |
| ■ *Corticosteroids and other Hormones* | cortisone acetate | Cortone |
| | estrogen | Evex, Menrium, Femest |
| | progesterone and derivatives | Lipo-Lutin, Progestasert, Proluton |
| | prednisone | Various Brands |
| ■ *Antiparkinson Drugs* | levodopa and carbidopa | Sinemet |
| | levodopa | Dopar, Larodopa |
| | amantadine hydrochloride | Symmetrel |
| ■ *Antianxiety Drugs* | alprazolam and others | Valium (see Figure 21) |
| ■ *Birth Control Pills* | progesterone estrogen | Various Brands |
| ■ *Alcohol* | wine, beer, spirits | Various Brands |
| ■ *Antivirals* | interferon, ribavirin | Reforon-A, Interon-A |
| ■ *Dermatological* | isotretinoin | Sotret, Amnesteem |
| ■ *Gastrointestinal* | metroclopramide | Reglan |

*Figure 3*

## SYMPTOMS COMMON TO ALL DEPRESSIONS

■ Mood of sadness, despair, emptiness

■ Anhedonia (loss of the ability to experience pleasure and a loss of interest in normal life activities)[1]

■ Low self-esteem

■ Apathy, low motivation, and social withdrawal

■ Excessive emotional sensitivity

■ Negative, pessimistic thinking

■ Irritability and low frustration tolerance

■ Suicidal ideas

■ Excessive guilt

■ Indecisiveness

---

[1]*Note:* Some degree of decreased capacity for pleasure may be seen in all types of depression. In severe depressions and in those that involve a biochemical disturbance, this loss of ability to experience pleasure can become so pronounced that the patient has almost no moments of joy or pleasure. Such people are said to have a "non-reactive mood," which means that they are unable to temporarily get out of their depressed mood.

## Figure 4

**VEGETATIVE/PHYSIOLOGICAL SYMPTOMS REFLECTING**
**A BIOCHEMICAL DYSFUNCTION**
(PRIMARY TARGET SYMPTOMS FOR MEDICATION TREATMENT)

- Sleep disturbance (early morning awakening, decreased sleep efficiency, frequent awakenings throughout the night,[1] occasionally hypersomnia: excessive sleeping)
- Appetite disturbance (decreased or increased, with accompanying weight loss or gain)
- Fatigue
- Chronic systemic inflammation (often accompanied by increased abdominal fat)
- Decreased sex drive
- Restlessness, agitation, or psychomotor retardation
- Diurnal variations in mood (usually feeling worse in the morning)
- Impaired concentration and forgetfulness
- Pronounced anhedonia (total loss of the ability to experience pleasure)

---

[1]*Note:* Initial insomnia (difficulty in falling asleep) may be seen with depression but is not diagnostic of a major depressive disorder. Initial insomnia can be seen in anyone experiencing stress in general. Initial insomnia alone is more characteristic of anxiety disorders than of depression.

medication treatment. However, if there is continuing weight loss, marked fatigue each day, and poor sleep most nights, antidepressants are indicated. In the Appendix we have included a brief symptom checklist that can be used to quickly assess a host of psychiatric symptoms. Depressive symptoms are included under Section A. Additionally, those patients who are depressed and are judged to be poor psychotherapy candidates (e.g., lower intelligence, not psychologically minded, or those who refuse psychotherapy) should be considered for a trial on antidepressants.

## Choosing Medication

Antidepressant medications fall into two primary groups: (1) typical antidepressants, and (2) MAO inhibitors. Empirical studies suggest that certain symptomatic presentations may point toward preferred first-line medication choices. This has resulted in the development of treatment guidelines. If the clinical picture is dominated by: anxiety, agitation, obsessional symptoms, rumination, irritability, aggression, and/or pronounced suicidality, serotonin reuptake inhibitors are the first-line treatment strategy (see Figure 5: those drugs indicated with an *). If the clinical picture is characterized by: apathy, low energy, anhedonia, and/or low motivation, dopamine or noradrenergic reuptake inhibitors are preferred (e.g., bupropion). (NIMH, 2002; Goodwin and Jamison, 2007)

A second major factor in choosing an antidepressant is the side effect profile (side effects are described in figure 5 and on page 12).

## Figure 5

## ANTIDEPRESSANT MEDICATIONS

| NAMES GENERIC | BRAND | USUAL DAILY DOSAGE RANGE | SEDATION | ACH EFFECTS[1] |
|---|---|---|---|---|
| *TYPICAL ANTIDEPRESSANTS* | | | | |
| desipramine | Norpramin | 150–300 mg | low | low |
| amitriptyline | Elavil | 150–300 mg | high | high |
| nortriptyline | Aventyl, Pamelor | 75–125 mg | mid | mid |
| trazodone | Oleptro | 150–400 mg | mid | none |
| fluoxetine* | Prozac, Sarafem | 20–80 mg | low | none |
| bupropion | Wellbutrin | 150–300 mg | low | none |
| sertraline* | Zoloft | 50–200 mg | low | none |
| paroxetine* | Paxil | 20–50 mg | low | low |
| venlafaxine | Effexor | 75–350 mg | low | none |
| desvenlafaxine | Pristiq | 50–300 mg | low | none |
| nefazodone | Serzone[2] | 100–500 mg | mid | low |
| fluvoxamine* | Luvox | 50–300 mg | low | low |
| mirtazapine | Remeron | 15–45 mg | mid | mid |
| citalopram* | Celexa | 10–40 mg | low | none |
| escitalopram* | Lexapro | 5–20 mg | low | none |
| duloxetine | Cymbalta | 20–80 mg | low | none |
| atomoxetine | Strattera[4] | 60–120 mg | low | low |
| vilazodone | Viibryd | 10–40 mg | low | none |
| vortioxetine | Trintellix | 10–20 mg | low | low |
| levomilnacipran | Fetzima | 40–120 mg | low | low |
| *MAO INHIBITORS*[3] | | | | |
| phenelzine | Nardil | 30–90 mg | low | none |
| tranylcypromine | Parnate | 20–60 mg | low | none |
| selegiline | Emsam | 6–12 mg | low | none |
| *ATYPICAL ANTIDEPRESSANTS* | | | | |
| brexanolone | Zulresso[5] | | | |
| esketamine | Spravato[6] | | | |

---

[1]*ACH EFFECTS* (anticholinergic side effects) include dry mouth, constipation, difficulty in urinating, and blurry vision. Can cause confusion and memory disturbances in the elderly or brain-damaged patient.

[2]Due to short half-life, requires divided dosing. The brand name drug Serzone is no longer being manufactured.

[3]Require strict adherence to dietary and medication regimen. Emsam at a dose of 6 mg does not require dietary restrictions.

[4]Technically an antidepressant but mainly used to treat ADHD.

[5]This medication is administered IV over a period of 60 hours. See more extensive information on page 19.

[6]This medication is administered via nasal spray. Frequency of administration varies widely. See more extensive information on page 14.

*Note:* Prescribe bupropion to patients with history of seizures only with great caution.

*A widely prescribed class of antidepressants are the *selective serotonin reuptake inhibitors* (SSRIs), which include: fluoxetine, paroxetine, sertraline, fluvoxamine, citalopram, and escitalopram.

# Prescribing Treatment

Antidepressant medications are generally started at a low dosage and gradually titrated up. With depressed patients even slight side effects often lead to non-compliance. The most common mistake made by family physicians is to under-medicate. Although there are exceptions, generally a patient (ages 16–55) must receive a dose that is within the therapeutic range (see Figure 5). (Doses for those over 55 are often somewhat lower.)

Typical start-up regimens would be as follows:

| Drug | Brand Name | (doses for adults ages 16-55) Starting dose | Increase in 1-2 weeks, if tolerated |
|------|-----------|---------------------------|------------------|
| Fluoxetine | Prozac | 10 mg | 20 mg |
| Sertraline | Zoloft | 50 mg | 100 mg |
| Paroxetine | Paxil | 10 mg | 20 mg |
| Citalopram | Celexa | 20 mg | 40 mg |
| Venlafaxine | Effexor | 37.5 mg bid | 75 mg bid |
| Desvenlafaxine | Pristiq | 50 mg | 50–100 mg |
| Bupropion | Wellbutrin | 100 mg | 100 mg bid |
| Nefazodone | Generic only | 50 mg bid | 100 mg bid |
| Mirtazapine | Remeron | 15 mg | 30 mg |
| Escitalopram | Lexapro | 5 mg | 10 mg |
| Duloxetine | Cymbalta | 20 mg | 40 mg |
| Atomoxetine | Strattera[1] | 25 mg | 60 mg |
| Vilazodone | Viibryd | 10 mg | 20–30 mg |
| Vortioxetine | Trintellix | 10 mg | 20 mg |
| Levomilnacipran | Fetzima | 20 mg | 40 mg |

[1]Atomoxetine is technically an antidepressant (NRI: norepinephrine reuptake inhibitor) but it is only approved by the FDA for treating ADHD.

Increases in dose can be made if there is a failure to show a positive response after 4–5 weeks of treatment. Note: If the patient had first episode prior to the age of 18, is experiencing a recurrent episode, and/or has been depressed for more than two months, this often requires 4–6 weeks to show first signs of a clinical response.

The treatment of major depression involves three phases:

*Acute Treatment:* Begins with the first dose and extends until the patient is asymptomatic (in good case scenarios, this may be from 6–8 weeks but often takes longer).

*Continuation Treatment:* To avoid acute relapse, it is strongly suggested that patients continue treatment for a minimum of six months beyond the acute phase. Also, recent studies indicate that the patient should be maintained on the *same* dose used during the acute phase.

*Maintenance Treatment:* Relapse prevention is an important aspect of treatment, especially in those patients judged to have recurrent episodes (or at risk for recurrence).* Research has shown that subsequent episodes tend to be more

*Note:* 70–80% of patients with major depression will experience either chronic or recurrent, episodic depressions.

## Figure 6

## DECISION TREE FOR DIAGNOSIS
## AND TREATMENT OF DEPRESSION - I

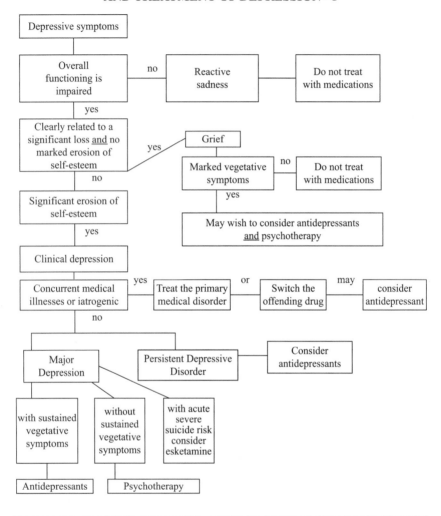

severe and resistant to treatment. Continued (lifelong) treatment provides the best outcome for such individuals. Chronic treatment may protect many individuals from subsequent episodes, although most patients suffering from recurrent major depression will experience some additional episodes (albeit, with decreased frequency and severity). The following guidelines are offered:

1. *First Episode:* At the end of the continuation phase, gradually reduce the dose (over a period of 4–6 weeks to avoid acute discontinuation withdrawal symptoms) and, assuming no return of depressive symptoms, discontinue. Educate the patient to be alert

*Figure 6 (cont.)*

## DECISION TREE: TREATMENT OF DEPRESSION - II

**Phase of Treatment**

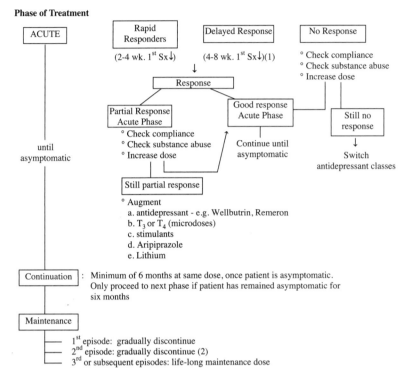

Footnotes:
1. Patients with the following characteristics may ultimately be good responders, but take longer to achieve first signs of symptomatic improvement: current episode has been ongoing for more than three months and the symptoms are severe.
2. If a second episode and these risk factors are present, may consider life-long treatment: first episode was prior to the age of 18, family history of mood disorders, inter-episode the patient was not euthymic (i.e., did not fully recover from first episode).
3. This decision tree is based on results from the Texas Medication Algorithm Project (1998) and A. John Rush (1997). Note that the general concepts from the project are addressed in this decision-tree, however, the particular graphics above were developed by the authors of this book.

to any signs of recurrence (e.g., poor sleep, fatigue, etc.) and should this occur, contact the treating health care professional as soon as possible to reinstigate treatment.

2. *Second Episode:*

   a. With "*Risk Factors*" which include family history of mood disorders, first episode occurring prior to the age of 18, and/or most recent episode has severe symptoms: Recommend life-long medication treatment to prevent recurrence.

   b. Without "*Risk Factors*": gradually discontinue medications.

3. *Third or later episodes.* Recommend life-long medication treatment.

## Figure 7

### SPECIAL PROBLEMS AND MEDICATIONS OF CHOICE

| THE PROBLEM | ALTERNATIVE MEDICATION CONSIDERATIONS |
|---|---|
| 1. High suicide risk[1] | 1. Avoid tricyclics, MAOIs; consider esketamine if the risk is very severe. |
| 2. Concurrent depression and panic attacks or OCD | 2. SSRIs |
| 3. Chronic pain with or without depression | 3. amitriptyline, nortriptyline, venlafaxine, duloxetine |
| 4. Weight gain on other antidepressants | 4. bupropion, SSRIs[2] avoid mirtazapine |
| 5. Sensitivity to anticholinergic side effects | 5. Avoid tricyclics and paroxetine |
| 6. Orthostatic hypotension | 6. nortriptyline, bupropion, sertraline |
| 7. Sexual dysfunction | 7. bupropion, nefazodone |
| 8. Anorexia/failure to thrive | 8. mirtazapine |
| 9. Drug interactions | 9. sertraline; citalopram |
| 10. Problematic withdrawal effects | 10. Recommend gradual withdrawal. Consider avoiding venlafaxine and paroxetine |
| 11. Pregnancy | 11. Avoid paroxetine |

[1]*Note:* Many older-generation antidepressants (e.g. tricyclics and MAO inhibitors) are quite toxic when taken in overdose. Extreme caution should be exercised in prescribing to high-risk suicidal patients.
[2]Weight gain is rare in the acute phase of treatment with SSRIs, however, with prolonged use approximately 10% of patients will experience noticeable weight gain.

## What to Expect

It has been hypothesized that many of the primary symptoms of clinical depression are caused by a dysregulation of certain neurotransmitters (e.g., norepinephrine, dopamine, and/or serotonin) and intracellular second messengers. Antidepressant medications are able to restore normal neurochemical functioning in key limbic structures in the brain. They have also been shown to increase the production of neuroprotective proteins (e.g. BDNF) and reduce levels of stress hormones (e.g. cortisol). It is very important to note, however, that these drugs do not act rapidly. It generally requires 2–4 weeks of treatment for symptoms to *begin* to improve. This is a crucial point. Many, if not most, depressed patients become easily discouraged if there is no relief in a few days. Such patients often discontinue medications prematurely.

## Side Effects

Probably owing to their tremendous feelings of hopelessness and pessimism, depressed patients are especially prone to discontinuing treatment prematurely.

This is often the case when they encounter side effects which typically emerge long before the therapeutic effects are realized. Thus, choosing medications that are low in side effects is an important rule of thumb. Fortunately, most newer generation antidepressants have a far better side effect profile than older generation tricyclics.

### Figure 8

**Drop-outs due to side effects**
**First six weeks of treatment**

| | |
|---|---|
| Placebo | 3–7% |
| Tricyclics | 25–30% |
| New generation antidepressants | 9–21% |

Side effects certainly account for treatment failures, however, it should be noted that other factors also contribute to treatment drop-outs (see Figure 8). It is likely that many drop-outs are due to the prolonged time before the onset of symptomatic improvement and tremendous pessimism that is a cardinal feature of depression.

## Side Effect Management Considerations: SSRIs and SNRIs

SSRIs and SNRIs are judged to be very effective medications for the treatment of depression presenting with agitation and/or co-morbid anxiety. However, many patients experience an increase in anxiety, restlessness, and/or insomnia during the first week or two of treatment (i.e. this is referred to as activation and is a common acute side effect which may emerge several hours after taking the first dose of an SSRI or soon after increasing the dose). This side effect can be *very* problematic in that it often leads to patient-initiated discontinuation. Typically this side effect diminishes in 2–3 weeks. An often-effective solution is to begin treatment by co-administering a low dose of a minor tranquilizer (e.g. 0.25–0.5 mg lorazepam, bid or tid) to be used only for the first month of treatment, and then discontinued. This not only controls drug-induced activation but can also provide very quick relief from anxiety if co-morbid anxiety is a part of the clinical picture. The rapid decrease in anxiety is often experienced by the patient as a very positive sign that medication treatments can be helpful and may inspire hope to continue taking medications until the more prominent antidepressant actions begin to emerge. If the only manifestation of activation is initial insomnia, then the use of the sedating antidepressant, trazodone (e.g., 50–75 mg qhs) or mirtazapine (Remeron, 7.5-15 mg qhs) are popular and effective strategies. Trazodone or Remeron are also drugs of choice for initial insomnia in patients where there is a history or suspected problem of substance abuse (they are non-habit-forming).

SSRIs and SNRIs are widely prescribed for depression owing to their effectiveness and relatively low incidence of side effects. Three late-onset side effects (generally seen several months into treatment) have been noted. These side effects are a common reason for patient-initiated discontinuation or poor compliance, and are side effects patients seldom report (thus, it is important for the physician to inquire). Sexual dysfunction (primarily inorgasmia) occurs as a side effect in 25-30% of patients taking SSRIs or other antidepressants that have significant serotonergic actions (i.e. venlafaxine, nefazodone, mirtazapine) (Clayton, et al. 2002). Please note that the base rate for sexual dysfunction (SD) in the general population is rather high and is also a common symptom of depression. Thus various causes of SD are commonly seen in depressed patients (however, the main type of SD seen as an antidepressant *side effect* is inorgasmia). Impotence is rare as a side effect. Interestingly, sildenafil (Viagra), which was developed to treat male erectile dysfunction, has been used successfully to combat drug-induced inorgasmia in both men and women. A second late-onset side effect is decreased spontaneity and apathy. This side effect may be spotted by reports by the patient that "I'm feeling depressed again." However, on closer inspection most depressive symptoms continue to be in remission. Rather, the patient is experiencing either a loss of motivation or a decreased sense of emotional aliveness (sometimes including an inability to cry). The third late-onset side effect is weight gain (which apparently is not associated with increased caloric intake, and affects about 10% of patients on chronic SSRI or SNRI treatment). Note that since many people suffering from depression may experience the symptom of weight loss, with successful resolution of the depression, they may regain lost weight. This is a consequence of recovery, not weight gain as a side effect.

*Figure 9*

| PROBLEM | TREATMENT OPTION |
|---|---|
| ■ Inorgasmia | ■ Reduce SSRI dose, or<br>■ Sildenafil (50–100 mg., p.r.n.)<br>■ Add bupropion |
| ■ Apathy, decreased spontaneity | ■ Reduce SSRI dose, or<br>■ Add bupropion (start low: e.g., 75 mg. b.i.d. and do not exceed 300 mg. q.d.)<br>■ Add 10-20 mg am dose of methylphenidate |
| ■ Weight gain | ■ Exercise and dieting |

These side effects can often be successfully managed by the solutions indicated above:

## Common Treatment Errors to Avoid

- Under-dosing
- Poor compliance
- Misdiagnosis: especially problematic if the patient actually has bipolar disorder. Antidepressants in bipolar patients may provoke manic episodes and/or increase frequency of episodes.
- Co-morbid substance abuse; especially moderate-to-heavy alcohol use (if not detected, can result in treatment failure of antidepressants. This is a very common reason for inadequate medication response).

- Longer-term use of benzodiazepines to treat depression (can increase depressive symptoms and may lead to drug dependence/abuse)
- Premature discontinuation
- Rapid discontinuation (especially troublesome with venlafaxine and paroxetine)

## Esketamine, Psilocybin, and Beyond

The drug ketamine has been used in medicine and veterinary medicine for years as an anesthetic. It also has been abused as a street drug, because of its dissociative and hallucinogenic properties (on the street often referred to as Special K). It is also widely used in psychiatry mainly in ketamine clinics to treat severe, treatment refractory depression and especially acute, severe suicide risk. In psychiatry it is used off label and administered typically twice a week in the clinic, because it requires IV dosing and a period of 2-3 hours of patient observation afterwards. This is because dissociative and some psychotic symptoms exist for a period of several hours after dosing. Some severely affected patients respond rapidly to antidepressants effects, often with a rapid decrease in suicidal ideas and impulses. It has also been used successfully to treat patients with psychotic depressive episodes.

Recently the active S isomer of ketamine (esketamine; brand name Spravato) has been FDA approved to treat depression and acute suicidal risk. It is available in a nasal spray. Because of its abuse potential, it is tightly regulated by both pharmacies and treatment facilities. It must be administered in the treatment facility. The current cost ranges from $4500-$6500 per month, but because it is FDA approved, it may be covered by insurance. The duration of effects and even the frequency of dosing is largely unknown. S-ketamine is a glutamate NMDA antagonist, although its specific mechanism of action is largely unknown. In many individuals the effects are seen within minutes to hours. The success of S-ketamine opens the door for future drug development because its action on glutamate is clearly different than other, standard antidepressants.

Psilocybin is a psychedelic drug that is found in certain mushrooms. The drug's hallucinogenic properties have made it a popular recreational drug of abuse for decades. It has also been an important part of religious ceremonies of various indigenous groups of the Americas. However, researchers now believe that psilocybin may be an effective intervention for treatment-resistant depression (defined as failure to respond to at least two antidepressants from different drug classes). Research in animal studies point to possible new and stronger neuronal connections as a result of psilocybin use, which may lead to reductions in depression and chronic stress. Recent clinical trials in humans indicate significant improvement in symptoms of treatment-resistant depression when combined with psychotherapy. These same trials, however, have raised safety concerns as increased suicidal ideation may be a side effect of higher doses of the drug. Although initial results are promising, it is too early to tell if the psychoactive component of "magic mushrooms" will become commonplace in depression treatment.

# KEY POINTS TO COMMUNICATE TO PATIENTS

In prescribing antidepressant medication, patient education is especially important. Listed below are the key points to communicate to patients starting on antidepressants.

1. Onset of clinical action generally takes 2–4 weeks. It will take this long for you to notice the onset of reduction of symptoms.

2. Symptomatic improvement is usually seen primarily in the physiological symptoms (Figure 4). Many of the other symptoms (e.g., depressed mood, low self-esteem, etc.) may respond only partially to medication treatment. These medications are not "happy pills"; they do not totally erase feelings of sadness or emptiness.

3. The best barometers of early medication response generally include improved sleep, less daytime fatigue, and some improvement in emotional control (e.g., less frequent crying spells or better frustration tolerance). The prescriber may need to inquire specifically about these symptoms because many depressed people will say "I'm no better," despite the fact that there are subtle signs of symptomatic improvement.

4. There may be side effects. However, side effects can most often be managed by dosage adjustment or by switching to another medication.

5. Total length of treatment varies considerably for individuals. Typically, it may take 6–8 weeks for the major depressive symptoms to subside. It is very important not to discontinue treatment at this point. The acute relapse rate can be as high as 50+%. The general rule of thumb is to continue treatment for a period of 6 months beyond the point of symptomatic improvement and then gradually to reduce the dose. Should symptoms return during this medication-reduction phase of treatment, the dosage should again be increased. Medication should be continued for 2–3 months before another trial on lower doses. Occasionally, a person may need to be on long-term chronic medication management.

6. Antidepressants are not addictive.

7. You should not drink alcohol when taking antidepressants. Alcohol can block the effects of the antidepressants (although, in clinical practice, many prescribers will allow patients on antidepressants to have an occasional drink, but not in excess of one per day).

8. Never discontinue "cold turkey"; this can result in withdrawal symptoms. Withdrawal symptoms can include nausea, anxiety, insomnia, flu-like general malaise and sometimes a peculiar sensation described by patients as "electrical shocks" experienced in the limbs or the head.

9. Two strategies always improve depression: exercise and a reduction of substances that impair sleep (most common: caffeine and alcohol).

## If First Line Medications Do Not Lead to Remission

Common treatment failures are often due to:

a. Misdiagnosis: e.g. patient has bipolar disorder, uncomplicated bereavement, or conditions better addressed with psychotherapy.

b. Missing common, unsuspected medical co-morbidities:

    a. Obstructive sleep apnea

b. Restless legs syndrome
c. Sleep disturbances due to excessive use of caffeine and/or alcohol
d. Sub-clinical hypothyroid: in those currently clinically depressed very slight elevations in TSH can significantly exacerbate depression or render treatments ineffective (e.g. TSH levels in the 1.5-3.0 range). Such levels are clearly in the normal range for most individuals, except for those in the throes of a severe depression. In such cases very small doses of thyroid replacement hormones can be helpful, with the goal to gradually reduce TSH levels to 1.0 (the optimal level for those with active depressive disorder). This has been found to be a very successful intervention for partial or poor responders who are depressed.

Beyond these considerations, generally it is best to start with a typical antidepressant. It is necessary to treat at adequate doses; many treatment failures are due to inadequate doses. Unless side effects are intolerable or a person is a high-risk patient (see *Precautions,* p. 17), standard practice is to gradually push the dose to the upper level of the therapeutic range until symptomatic improvement is attained. This strategy was borne out in a large-scale study (STAR-D program) supported by the National Institute of Mental Health. The best results were achieved beginning with standard doses (see table on page 8). If there was a failure to respond by week four doses were gradually increased (e.g. Celexa: 60 mg.; Effexor: 375 mg; Wellbutrin: 400 mg . . . unless side effects prohibited this). Failure to use high enough dosing is a common reason for lack of response. In this study, those who experienced significant improvement or remission generally did so within 7 weeks. If a patient is on a high dose for a period of 4–6 weeks without symptomatic improvement, it is unlikely that improvement will occur. If there is a partial response, then a strategy that is often successful is to augment. The most common forms of augmentation are: SSRI plus bupropion (e.g. 150-400 mg qd), T3, 25-50 micrograms qd, SSRI plus low dose stimulant (e.g. methylphenidate, 5-10 mg) especially for depressions accompanied by marked fatigue and apathy, buspirone (15-40 mg qd) especially for depressions with co-morbid anxiety symptoms, addition of the antipsychotics aripiprazole and brexpiprazole (note: these medications have FDA approval for augmenting antidepressant treatment in non-psychotic depressions; they also can treat psychotic symptoms), or antidepressant plus low doses of lithium (e.g., 600-900 mg qd). A fairly large number of non-respondents do benefit from augmentation. Should this fail, then a change in the antidepressant medication is in order.

The next step generally is to switch to another typical antidepressant. The choice is guided by two factors: side effect profiles and neurotransmitter action. There is some evidence to suggest that there exist three basic neurochemicals that may be affected in major depressive disorder: norepinephrine, dopamine and serotonin. The various antidepressant medications have different effects on these three neurochemical systems (see Figure 10). Some are considered to have broad spectrum effects ("shotguns") and others are more selective ("bullets"). If your first unsuccessful drug was serotonergic, then the second choice should be a medication targeting norepinephrine or dopamine.

What if this fails too? The next strategy is to switch to mirtazanine, venlafaxine, duloxetine, or to an MAO inhibitor. Treatment is described below. The final option is electroconvulsive therapy (ECT), which is a highly effective, albeit costly, form of treatment for depression.

## Figure 10

### SELECTIVE ACTION OF ANTIDEPRESSANT MEDICATIONS[1]

| GENERIC | BRAND | NOREPINEPHRINE NE | SEROTONIN 5-HT | MONOAMINE OXIDASE | DOPAMINE DA |
|---|---|---|---|---|---|
| desipramine | Norpramin | +++++ | 0 | 0 | 0 |
| amitriptyline | Elavil | ++ | ++++ | 0 | 0 |
| nortriptyline | Aventyl, Pamelor | +++ | ++ | 0 | 0 |
| venlafaxine | Effexor | ++ | +++ | 0 | + |
| desvenlafaxine | Pristiq | ++ | +++ | 0 | + |
| trazodone | Oleptro | 0 | +++++ | 0 | 0 |
| fluoxetine | Prozac | 0 | +++++ | 0 | 0 |
| paroxetine | Paxil | + | +++++ | 0 | 0 |
| sertraline | Zoloft | 0 | +++++ | 0 | + |
| bupropion | Wellbutrin[2] | +++ | 0 | 0 | ++ |
| nefazodone | Serzone | + | ++++ | 0 | 0 |
| fluvoxamine | Luvox | 0 | +++++ | 0 | 0 |
| mirtazapine | Remeron | ++ | +++ | 0 | 0 |
| citalopram | Celexa | 0 | +++++ | 0 | 0 |
| escitalopram | Lexapro | 0 | +++++ | 0 | 0 |
| duloxetine | Cymbalta | ++++ | ++++ | 0 | 0 |
| atomoxetine | Strattera | +++++ | 0 | 0 | 0 |
| vilazodone | Viibryd | 0 | +++++ | 0 | 0 |
| vortioxetine | Trintellix | + | +++++ | 0 | + |
| levomilnacipran | Fetzima | +++ | +++ | 0 | 0 |
| phenelzine | Nardil[3] | +++ | +++ | +++++ | +++ |
| tranylcypromine | Parnate[3] | +++ | +++ | +++++ | +++ |
| isocarboxacid | Marplan[3] | +++ | +++ | +++++ | +++ |
| selegiline | Emsam | +++ | +++ | +++++ | +++ |
| brexanolone | Zulresso[4] | | | | |
| esketamine | Spravato[4] | | | | |

[1] 0 = no impact on neurotransmitter; + = minimal impact, +++++ = significant impact.
[2] Atypical antidepressant.
[3] MAOIs increase NE, 5-HT, and DA.
[4] Presumed mechanisms of action are discussed on pages 14 and 19.

*Note* that the clinician must wait 2 weeks after discontinuing typical antidepressants before beginning an MAOI, and six weeks after discontinuing fluoxetine before a switch to an MAOI. Failure to do so may result in very serious and potentially life-threatening drug interactions.

## Persistent Depressive Disorder (DSM-5, formerly known as dysthymia)

Dysthymia is a type of mild, chronic depressive disorder characterized by the following symptoms (which are present almost every day over a period of 2+ years):

- Daytime fatigue
- Negative, pessimistic thinking
- Low self-esteem
- Low motivation, loss of enthusiasm
- Decreased capacity for joy

Evidence from a number of studies suggests that approximately two-thirds of patients with dysthymia can respond favorably to a trial on anti-depressant medications. MAOIs and SSRIs appear to be more effective than tricyclics in treating dysthymia.

## Major Depression with Atypical Symptoms

15–20% of major depressions present with what are referred to as *atypical symptoms,* which include: hypersomnia (excessive sleeping), significant weight gain, carbohydrate craving, and extreme fatigue. It is important to note that this is the most common clinical presentation of depression in patients with bipolar illness. As will be addressed in the next chapter, treatment of bipolar depression with antidepressants alone carries risks of precipitating a shift into mania and/or cycle acceleration. Thus the clinician must always take special note of atypical symptoms and be cautious about treating with antidepressants (see chapter 3 for more details). Atypical symptoms are also the most common presentation seen in seasonal affective disorder.

## Seasonal Affective Disorder (S.A.D.)

Decreased exposure to photic stimulation has been strongly implicated in cases of S.A.D. This is often a factor in people who work at night, live in geographic areas with significant cloud cover and/or pollution, and in northern climes (Northern hemisphere) during winter months. A full discussion of S.A.D. is beyond the scope of this book, but prescribers should be aware of this common clinical condition. Treatment for S.A.D. includes antidepressants (current hypotheses suggest that S.A.D. may be closely tied to serotinergic dysfunction, and thus SSRIs may be medications of choice). Additionally, increased bright light exposure has been shown to be effective (either by use of commercially available light boxes or by encouraging patients to spend a minimum of one hour per day outside . . . of course, without sunglasses). Since many cases of seasonal depression are a manifestation of bipolar disorder, please note that increased bright light exposure can precipitate manias in those with bipolar illness.

For a detailed discussion of S.A.D., please see *Winter Blues* by N.E. Rosenthal, Guilford Press, N.Y. (2012).

## Pre-menstrual Dysphoric Disorder (PMDD)

Approximately 5% of women experience severe mood changes premenstrually. This disorder is characterized by the tremendous regularity of mood symptoms (depression, irritability or anxiety) seen for a few days prior to menstruation. Serotinergic dysregulation has been implicated and treatment with SSRIs is often a successful strategy. Currently, there is some debate whether or not it is necessary to treat PMDD continuously (i.e., all month-long) or on a P.R.N. basis. All other types of depression require chronic treatment, however; some women with PMDD *may* respond to P.R.N. dosing only during the symptomatic time of the month.

## Postpartum Depression

Clinically significant postpartum depression can affect up to 10-14% of women giving birth. Technically, this can occur during pregnancy but more commonly after. Especially if there is a pre-existing depression, the onset can follow rapidly after delivery. However, more commonly, the average onset is 6 weeks following delivery. Postpartum depression is distinct from what often is referred to as "the baby blues." Such a condition is not pathological but rather reflects increased emotional sensitivity in general (for the full range of emotions, including happiness as well as bouts of sadness or tearfulness). It is thought that this phenomenon, common to most new mothers, is adaptive in its contribution to increased empathy, nurturing and mother child bonding. Postpartum depression is quite different.

Postpartum depression often manifests as moderate to extremely severe. Its typical onset around 6 weeks has raised questions about the adverse impact of sleep deprivation, especially during the first weeks or months following delivery. Technically, severe depression with onset during the first year after giving birth to a baby may be a manifestation of postpartum depression. This condition, beyond causing significant suffering for the mother, can be quite severe and often quite risky. Many women experiencing a severe episode are completely unable to or uninterested in holding their babies, profoundly interfering with critical early child-mother bonding (consequences that may have a life-long impact). The greatest risk is postpartum psychosis. Here mothers do not interact at all with their children and in many include the child in delusional thinking. Estimates show that each year in the United States 150 babies are killed by their mothers in the midst of florid psychotic thinking and behavior. All women with postpartum psychosis should be strongly considered for hospitalization.

The standard in practice for many years is the combined use of antidepressants and antipsychotics (especially if psychotic symptoms are present). Response rates are slow and such depressive and psychotic symptoms (if untreated) last longer than most unipolar depressive episodes. They may continue for 1.5 or more years or more before spontaneous remission. Standard treatment requires at least 2-4 weeks to begin to respond.

Brexanolone (brand name Zulresso) is a new drug with unique actions. It requires gradual IV infusion over a period of 60 hours and must be administered in the hospital. This is the first FDA approved drug for postpartum depression. It is presumed to have actions on allopregnanolone, a neuro-steroid that has actions on the GABA system. Both with premenstrual depression and postpartum depressions allopregnanolone levels drop precipitously. Progesterone may be targeted by the drug but the precise mechanism of action is unknown at the time of this printing. Typically, 30% of women experience a significant and rapid reduction in psychiatric symptoms. The drug may have enduring positive effects for at least a month, but longer-term follow-up studies have not been done to date. Also, most patients must be co-treated with antidepressants and possibly antipsychotics during and after brexanolone treatment.

The cost of the medication alone is currently $34,000, which does not include the cost of the hospital stay and the clinicians involved. Since it is FDA approved, it may be reimbursed by some insurance companies. The cost is very high, however this condition should be considered potentially life-threatening, which may justify the cost. The most common side effect is dizziness.

Like all new drugs with totally unique action, such drug development may pave the way for development of other compounds. A pill form is currently under investigation.

## Psychotic Depressions

Psychotic symptoms may be seen in cases of unipolar depression and bipolar disorder, and occur also in the context of postpartum and menopausal depressions. They usually manifest with severe vegetative symptoms, delusions (especially somatic delusions, extreme beliefs regarding worthlessness, and paranoid thinking) and occasionally, auditory hallucinations.

Antidepressants alone or antipsychotics alone are generally ineffective. Almost always the treatment of choice includes a combination of antidepressants and antipsychotics. Electroconvulsive therapy (E.C.T.) may be both necessary and effective in more severe cases. Finally, please keep in mind that these patients are very high risk for suicide. Referral to a psychopharmacologist (e.g., psychiatrist, prescribing/medical psychologist, psychiatric nurse practitioner) and possibly hospitalization are required.

## Precautions: Tricyclic Antidepressants

The following patients should either not be treated or treated cautiously with tricyclics: immediate post-myocardial infarction patients, epileptics, patients with narrow-angle glaucoma, and pregnant women. The prescriber should consult package inserts and the *Physicians' Desk Reference* for more details regarding precautions and contraindications.

Very low doses of nortriptyline (e.g. 10-40 mg) or amitriptyline (e.g. 10-50 mg) offer a good alternative to opiates to reduce pain. At these doses, these antidepressants are not high enough dose to treat depression and are not habit forming.

## Precautions: Selective Serotonin Reuptake Inhibitors and Serotonin and Norepinephrine Reuptake Inhibitors (SNRIs)

Drug-drug interactions can sometimes be dangerous. SSRIs and SNRIs should be used *cautiously* with certain medications (Figure 11). Also note that very rare cases of liver toxicity have been reported with the antidepressants nefazodone and atomoxetine.

## Precautions: Watch for Bipolar Disorder

Patients with a personal or family history of bipolar disorder often present with depressive symptoms. They may or may not reveal a history of mania. Caution should be exercised in prescribing since all antidepressants can precipitate a shift from depression into mania. It is always advisable to ask the patient (and family members) if there has been a family history of bipolar illness (see Chapter 3) or if any of the following symptoms of possible hypomania have been present for more than one or two days:

- Decreased need for sleep, but without daytime fatigue
- Rapid, pressured speech
- High levels of energy
- Intense irritability
- Racing thoughts

### *Figure 11*

- ■ MAO Inhibitors—never use with SSRIs (very dangerous/fatal)
- ■ Tricyclic antidepressants (may increase SSRI levels)
- ■ Lithium (SSRIs may increase lithium levels)
- ■ Carbamazepine (SSRIs may increase carbamazepine levels)
- ■ St. John's Wort (may be dangerous)
- ■ The use of the over-the-counter product 5-HTP along with SSRIs and SNRIs can result in a serotonin sydrome and can be dangerous

*Note:* This list is not exhaustive, but includes common drug-drug interactions

In addition, any of the following may suggest the depressive phase of bipolar disorder: a history of relatively brief major depressions (less than 3 months), a history of a first-onset major depression prior to age 18; psychotic symptoms (e.g. delusions); unsuccessful past treatments with antidepressants (despite adequate trials) or a positive response lasting only a month or two, with a return of depressive symptoms; clear seasonal patterns to depressions (i.e. history of depressions occurring in the winter); and/or the presence of atypical symptoms (as described on page 15).

If a patient presents with any of these characteristics, they should be considered bipolar until proven otherwise.

## MAO Inhibitors

Three commonly used MAOIs (phenelzine, selegiline and tranylcypromine) have been shown to be as effective as tricyclics in a number of studies. However, shortly after their introduction into the United States in the 1950s there were reports of severe reactions in some patients, which resulted in great concern in the medical community. The drugs interact with certain medications (sympathomimetic amines) and with certain foods (containing tyramine, a natural byproduct of bacterial fermentation processes, found in many cheeses, some wines and beers, and foods such as chopped liver, broad beans, chocolate, snails, etc.). (See Appendix B.) The interaction resulted in a severe hypertensive crisis, which for a number of patients was fatal. So for many years these medications were abandoned because doctors viewed them as unsafe. However, especially in Europe, doctors recognized that these drugs had clinical utility and could be safely used if certain dietary restrictions were followed. Additionally, the MAOI, Emsam (available in a transdermal patch) if given at a dose of 6 mg per day may not require dietary restrictions (such restrictions however may be necessary at doses of 9-12 mg).

MAOIs should be considered as a third or fourth-line treatment choice, should other antidepressants fail. Additionally, some studies indicate that MAOIs may be the drug of choice for some types of affective disorders including atypical depressions presenting primarily with anxiety and phobic symptoms, masked depression (e.g., hypochondriasis), highly treatment resistant depressions and dysthymia.

Otherwise, guidelines for treatment and clinical response are similar to those previously described for typical antidepressants. The one exception is the important dietary/medication restrictions that must be observed (see Appendix B, patient handout for specific restrictions).

## Notes on Over-the-Counter Products

Several over-the-counter products have been shown to have efficacy in treating depression. Please see chapter 7.

## Books to Recommend to Patients

1. Preston, J. and Kirk, M. (2011) *Depression 101.* New Harbinger Publishers, Oakland, CA.

2. Fast, J. and Preston, J. (2008) *Getting Things Done When You Are Depressed.* Alpha Books: New York.

# Chapter 3    Bipolar Illness

## DIAGNOSIS

## Major Clinical Features and Differential Diagnosis

The diagnosis of a bipolar disorder is based on two sources of data: the current clinical picture (depression or mania) and a clear history of both manic and depressive episodes. The depressive episodes may range from minor to major depressive syndromes as outlined in Chapter 2. Manic episodes typically are described as either full blown (Figure 14) or less intense manic episodes, referred to as hypomania.

It is important to rule out medical causes of bipolar illness. (See Figures 1 and 2 in Chapter 2 and Figures 12 and 13.)

*Figure 12*

### COMMON DISORDERS THAT MAY CAUSE MANIA

- Brain tumors
- CNS syphilis
- Delirium (due to various causes)
- Encephalitis
- Influenza
- Metabolic changes associated with hemodialysis
- Metastatic squamous adenocarcinoma
- Multiple sclerosis
- Q fever

*Figure 13*

### DRUGS THAT MAY CAUSE MANIA

- amphetamines
- bromides
- cocaine
- antidepressants
- isoniazid
- procarbazine
- steroids
- stimulants

DSM-5 is now being replaced in many clinical locations with ICD (International Classification of Diseases). The following are ICD diagnoses (note no Bipolar I or II):

Current episode, bipolar depression
Current episode, mania
Current episode with hypomania
Current episode, mixed states
Specifiers: Severity: mild, moderate, severe, and with psychotic symptoms

Several classification schemes for bipolar disorders have been proposed by various authors. The three most clinically useful classifications are outlined below:

## A. BIPOLAR I vs. BIPOLAR II

1. *Bipolar I*   This disorder fits the more classic description of bipolar illness with clearly recognized episodes of depression and mania.

2. *Bipolar II*   This disorder presents with obvious episodes of depression; but the manic phases of the illness are often brief, much less intense, unrecognized, and thus not reported by the patient. If you inquire about manic episodes, the patient will often give the impression that none have occurred. The best ways to diagnose such conditions are either to witness a hypomanic episode (see Figure 14) clinically or to carefully inquire about the history. In particular, if hypomanic episodes are suspected, the most important question to ask is, "Have you ever had a period of time when you didn't need as much sleep?" A decreased need for sleep and a lack of daytime fatigue are red flags for hypomania. Typical hypomanic episodes only last 4 or a few more days. Technically those experiencing hypomanias that last only 1-3 days are currently referred to as Short-Duration Depressive Episodes (DSM-5, 2013). These conditions have been considered to be a variant of bipolar disorder and should be treated as such. Many cases of apparent treatment-resistant depression may turn out to be bipolar II (they always present with depressive symptoms and many times do not respond well to treatments with antidepressants). Additionally, treatment with antidepressants alone can cause a shift into hypomania. Often it is very helpful to obtain information from a spouse or close relative; family members often clearly can identify a history of past hypomanias where patients cannot.

Note: ICD-10 classification of mental and behavioral disorders does not use the bipolar I and II nomenclature. Rather it lists the following types of episodes:

    a. Bipolar affective disorder, current episode hypomania

    b. Bipolar affective disorder, current episode manic

    c. Bipolar affective disorder, current episode depression

    d. Bipolar disorder affective disorder, current episode mixed

## B. TYPICAL BIPOLAR vs. RAPID CYCLING BIPOLAR DISORDERS

In the more typical bipolar patient, depressive and manic episodes last for several months, often with periods of normal mood occurring between periods of depression and mania. When there are two or more episodes of *both* depression and mania (e.g., depression-mania-depression-mania) within a year, this is referred to as "rapid cycling." Sometimes rapid cyclers (RC) can dramatically switch moods from week to week or even day to day. RC can best be seen as periods of exacerbation of bipolar disorder that are episodic (e.g. those who experience RC may do so for six months or a year, and then return to more typical episodes of mania and depression). Substance abuse or treatment with antidepressants are common factors in provoking RC and should always be evaluated in those with RC symptomatology.

## C. MANIA WITH MIXED FEATURES (DSM-5)

This is a diagnostic term which describes patients that have concurrent manic and depressive symptoms (e.g., increased activity or agitation, pressured speech, suicidal ideas, and feelings of worthlessness) (see Figure 14).

The subclassifications of Bipolar I and Bipolar II, typical vs. rapid cycling, and dysphoric mania are important because they have different treatment implications.

## Target Symptoms

The target symptoms vary depending on the current phase of the illness. Major depressive symptoms are listed in Chapter 2 (Figures 3 and 4). Manic episodes are identified by the following clinical features (see Figure 14).

# MEDICATIONS USED TO TREAT BIPOLAR ILLNESS

## When Do You Prescribe Medications?

Treatment of bipolar disorders has two goals. The first goal is the reduction of current symptoms, and the second is the prevention of relapse. Bipolar disorders are invariably recurring and thus prophylactic treatment is warranted. Although prevention of episode recurrence is a goal, in reality only about one in five will, with appropriate treatment, avoid subsequent episodes. The more common outcome is that appropriate treatment can significantly reduce the number and frequency of episodes. Unfortunately, even more common is that patients are non-compliant with medication treatment (typically owing to side effects) and the result is ongoing recurrences. Strong evidence indicates that failure to continue treatment can lead (and often does) not only to relapse, but to a progressively worsening condition. Subsequent episodes tend to become more and more severe and can, at times, become treatment refractory.

## Choosing Medication

An important medication used to treat this disorder is lithium (has the best track record providing long-term mood stabilization). Also it is important to note that several large-scale studies have shown that patients treated with lithium show a significant decrease in suicides (a 7-fold reduction in suicide rates). Thus although treatment with lithium can be challenging owing to the need for numerous blood tests and other types of laboratory monitoring, this drug continues to play an important role in the treatment of bipolar disorder. A number of other drugs have been found to be effective as adjuncts or alternatives to lithium. We will describe standard treatment with lithium and then comment on the role of other medications.

Lithium has two primary effects: It is used to treat acute mood episodes (i.e. it is used to treat acute manic and depressive episodes), and in many instances it can prevent relapse (or at least lessen the intensity of subsequent episodes) if treatment is on an ongoing basis. Lithium seems to be somewhat more effective in preventing relapse of mania rather than depression.

## Prescribing Treatment

The treatment of bipolar disorders can be quite complex. Generally a referral to a specialist is recommended, although recently there has been pressure on primary care physicians to treat this disorder.

## Figure 14

### SYMPTOMS OF MANIA[1]

- A pronounced and persistent mood of euphoria (elevated or expansive mood) or irritability and at least three of the following:
- Grandiosity or elevated self-esteem
- Decreased need for sleep
- Rapid, pressured speech (Often these people are hard, if not impossible, to interrupt.)
- Racing thoughts
- Distractibility
- Increased activity or psychomotor agitation
- Behavior that reflects expansiveness (lacking restraint in emotional expression) and poor judgment, such as increased sexual promiscuity, gambling, buying sprees, giving away money, etc.

### SYMPTOMS OF MIXED MANIA

- Marked irritability
- Severe agitation or anxiety
- Pessimism and unrelenting worry and despair
- Significant suicide risk
- Decreased need for sleep

### SYMPTOMS OF HYPOMANIA

- Increased energy and mental productivity
- Decreased need for sleep
- Talkative
- Elated, mildly grandiose
- Irritability

___

[1]See Questions 13–16 on the History and Personal Data Questionnaire (Appendix A.).

*If the presenting phase is a manic episode.* Often, especially if the patient is quite agitated, out of control or psychotic, the initial plan is to begin treatment with *both* an anti-manic agent and an antipsychotic medication (e.g., olanzapine). The anti-psychotics seem to improve behavioral control more rapidly. With most standard anti-manic medications, the patient may require 10 days to show a clinical response. Alternatively, high potency benzodiazepines can be used in place of anti-psychotics (e.g., clonazepam or lorazepam). Alprazolam (Xanax) can aggravate mania and should be avoided.

## Figure 15

### DECISION TREE FOR TREATMENT OF BIPOLAR DISORDERS

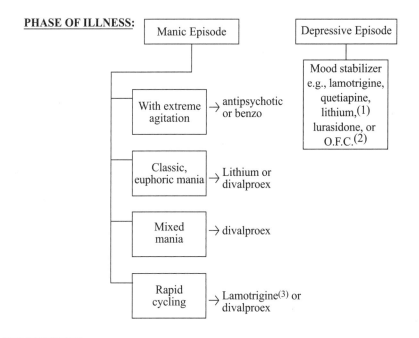

---

(1)To treat depression, lithium levels must reach or exceed 0.8 mEq/L.

(2)OFC: olanzapine-fluoxetine combination (Symbyax)

(3)Before treating rapid cycling check to see if the patient is abusing stimulants (e.g. methamphetamine) or is taking an antidepressant, as these often provoke rapid cycling. If these are discontinued, the use of additional bipolar medication may not be needed.

Treatment with lithium is initiated after necessary lab tests are conducted (see Figure 16). Generally the starting dose is 600 or 900 mg./day given in divided doses. The therapeutic range and toxic range of lithium are very close to one another. Thus it is necessary to gradually increase the dose while carefully monitoring blood levels. Most patients must reach a level between 1.0 and 1.2 mEq/L. Not infrequently the level may need to be higher to obtain symptomatic improvement (1.2 to 1.5), but on these higher levels, side effects are more common and compliance is poorer. On occasion, patients may need and tolerate blood levels up to 2.0 mEq/L. However, there is increased risk of toxicity at such doses. Generally, daily doses range from 1200-3000 mg. Once mood is adequately stabilized, the dose can be lowered somewhat (0.8 mEq/L blood level for Bipolar I or 0.6 mEq/L for Bipolar II) for maintenance treatment.

Major side effects include nausea, diarrhea, vomiting, fine hand tremor, sedation, muscular weakness, polyuria, polydypsia, edema, weight gain and a dry mouth. Adverse effects from chronic use may include leukocytosis (reversible upon discontinuation of lithium), hypothyroidism and goiter, acne, psoriasis, teratogenesis (first trimester, although the risk is very low), nephrogenic diabetes insipidus (reversible), and kidney damage.

Signs of toxicity include lethargy, ataxia, slurred speech, tinnitus, severe nausea/vomiting, tremor, arrhythmias, hypotension, seizures, shock, delirium, coma, and even death. Since the toxic range is near to the therapeutic range, blood levels and adverse effects must be monitored closely. In addition, a number of other clinical lab tests should be conducted at the beginning of treatment and periodically thereafter (see Figure 16).

## *Figure 16*

## CLINICAL LAB TESTS FOR PATIENTS TAKING LITHIUM

- NA (Sodium)
- Ca (Calcium)
- P (Phosphorus)
- EKG

- Creatinine
- Urinalysis
- Complete CBC
- Thyroid battery (with TSH)

Other antimanic agents can be used alone or in combination with lithium. These include: mood-stabilizing anticonvulsants: divalproex, carbamazepine, oxcarbazepine, or antipsychotics (all antipsychotics have potent antimanic effects). Most anticonvulsants have significant side effects and some are known teratogens. Common side effects include: nausea, fine hand tremor, sedation, weight gain (all except topiramate), rash, menstrual irregularities (please see PDR or package inserts for specific adverse effects associated with each of the anticonvulsant mood stabilizers). Generally the newer antipsychotics are used; e.g. olanzapine, risperidone, paliperidone, ziprasidone, quetiapine, or aripiprazole (see chapter 5 for more details on antipsychotic medications).

*If the presenting phase is a depressive episode.* Antidepressants alone in the treatment of bipolar depression may cause significant problems, by provoking a rapid shift into mania (and also may increase the subsequent frequency of episodes; i.e. causing cycle acceleration). Antidepressants as a monotherapy are not advised. Thus, typically the treatment of choice is to use one of the six following medications: cariprazine, lurasidone, lamotrigine, olanzapine-fluoxetine combination (OFC, brand name: Symbyax), quetiapine or lithium. Should this strategy fail, often a combination of two or more of these medications is effective. *Medication combinations are almost always necessary:* 90% of successfully treated bipolar patients require polypharmacy (e.g. lithium and quetiapine).

## Bipolar Disorder Medications:
### For Mania:

| Names | | Daily Dosage | Serum |
|---|---|---|---|
| Generic | Brand | Range (mg) | Level |
| lithium carbonate | Eskalith, Lithonate | 600–2400 | 0.6-1.5 mEq/l |
| carbamazepine | Tegretol, Equetro | 600–1200 | 4-10+ mcg/ml |
| divalproex | Depakote | 750–1500 | 50-125 mcg/ml |
| oxcarbazepine | Trileptal | 1200–2400 | 1 |

Note: All antipsychotic medications have antimanic properties
1: serum level not well established

**For Bipolar Depression**

| Generic | Names Brand | Daily Dosage Range (mg) |
|---|---|---|
| olanzapine-fluoxetine | Symbyax | 6/25-12-50 |
| quetiapine | Seroquel | 150-600 |
| lamotrigine | Lamictal | 50-500 |
| lurasidone | Latuda | 40-80 |
| cariprazine | Vraylar | 1-6 |

*Figure 17*

**SPECIALIZED TREATMENTS FOR SUBTYPES
OF BIPOLAR DISORDERS**

| SUBTYPE | MEDICATION ALTERNATIVES |
|---|---|
| Bipolar II | quetiapine (Seroquel) |
| | O-F-C (Symbyax) |
| | lurasidone (Latuda) |
| | lamotrigine (Lamictal) |
| | lithium with blood level at least 0.6 mEq/L |
| Mixed mania | divalproex (Depakote) |

One of the most common mistakes made in treating bipolar depression is the use of antidepressants, which can be problematic. They can cause switching from depression to mania, increase the frequency of episodes (of both mania and depression) and do not show efficacy. One exception is use of an antidepressant in treating treatment resistant Bipolar II depressions. The positive yield is only seen in about 25% of treatment-resistant Bipolar II disorders. General consensus is to use one or a combination of the medications listed above in Figure 17. These drugs show efficacy in treating bipolar depression. In addition, never use antidepressants in Bipolar I depression. The yield is very minimal and risks are significant. First line medication for depression in Bipolar II are the treatments of choice.

For details on alternative treatment approaches see the following:

*STEP-BD: Systematic Treatment Enhancement Program for Bipolar Disorder:
National Institute of Mental Health: http://www.stepbd.org and http://www.
psychiatryonline.org*

## Common Treatment Errors to Avoid

- Lithium: very toxic thus warrants close monitoring (especially in suicidal patients. *Note:* Suicides occur frequently not only in depressed but also manic patients). Acute dehydration can also result in toxic lithium levels.
- Poor compliance

- Discontinuation: *Note:* Bipolar patients need life-long treatment to avoid relapse. Patient or clinician-initiated discontinuation can and does result in frequent relapses. And, subsequent episodes often are more severe and may become treatment-resistant. If discontinuation must occur, it is strongly recommended that it be done gradually (e.g., over a period of 6 weeks).

# KEY POINTS TO COMMUNICATE TO PATIENTS

1. Lithium and other bipolar drugs are medications that treat your current emotional problem and will also be helpful in preventing relapse. So it will be important to continue with treatment after the current episode is resolved.

2. Since the therapeutic and toxic dosage ranges (lithium) are so close, we must monitor your blood level closely. Some anticonvulsant mood stabilizers also must have periodic monitoring. This will be done more frequently at first and every several months thereafter. Never increase your dose without first consulting with your physician.

3. Lithium and other bipolar medications are not addictive.

4. Many side effects can be reduced/minimized by taking divided doses or may subside as treatment progresses.

5. Bipolar disorders often run in families. Any relatives who have pronounced mood swings should be alerted to the possibility of a treatable condition and the need for professional evaluation. (The yield on this maneuver is high, since medical awareness of bipolar disorder is still low, especially with milder forms, and family history is impressively often positive for this disorder.)

6. You and your family need to be aware that this is a biological disorder, not a moral defect or a character flaw. When severe, you may not always be able to control your behavior, necessitating that practical steps be taken to protect all concerned from poor judgment during episodes.

7. Many self-help groups have been developed to provide support for bipolar patients and their families. In this community, the local self-help group is ____ , and you can find out more information by calling ____ .

8. Anticonvulsant mood stabilizers can cause birth defects so if you become pregnant or plan a pregnancy please contact your prescriber immediately.

9. Lifestyle management is especially important in maintaining stability. This cannot be overemphasized; without this critical ingredient, medication treatments often fail. Lifestyle management includes:

- Maintaining regular bedtimes and times for awakening
- Avoid sleep deprivation (even one night can be problematic)
- Avoid shift work
- Attempt to keep the amount of bright (sunlight) exposure stable throughout the year (note: decreased light exposure in the winter often provokes bipolar depression while excessive sunlight exposure in the summer often ignites mania).
- Avoid the use of alcohol and any illicit drug use
- Avoid substances that interfere with sleep: caffeine, alcohol, minor tranquilizers, decongestants, etc.
- If possible avoid or limit travel across time zones.

## Books to Recommend to Patients

1. Jamison, K. R. (1997). *Unquiet Mind,* Random House, New York.

2. Fast, J. and Preston, J. (2011) *Loving Someone with Bipolar Disorder*. New Harbinger Publications, Oakland, CA.

3. Fast, J. and Preston, J. (2006) *Taking Charge of Bipolar Disorder*. Warner Wellness Books. New York.

4. White, R. and Preston, J. (2010) *Bipolar Disorder 101.* New Harbinger Publications, Oakland, CA.

# Chapter 4  Anxiety Disorders

## DIAGNOSIS

## Major Clinical Features and Differential Diagnosis

Six different anxiety disorders are seen in clinical practice.[1] An accurate diagnosis is important as the treatments vary. There is no one treatment appropriate for all anxiety disorders. It is important to distinguish between the following: (1) generalized anxiety disorder (G.A.D.), (2) stress-related anxiety, (3) panic disorder, (4) social phobias, (5) medical illnesses presenting with anxiety symptoms, and (6) anxiety symptoms as a part of a primary mental disorder (e.g., depression, schizophrenia).

Before outlining the main features of each disorder, it is necessary to define two terms: panic attacks and anxiety symptoms. Panic attacks are very brief but extremely intense surges of anxiety. The major differences between a panic attack and more generalized anxiety symptoms are differences in the onset, duration, and intensity. Panic attacks often "come out of the blue" (i.e., not necessarily provoked by stress), they come on suddenly (the full attack reaching its peak in from one-to-ten minutes), are *extremely* intense, last from 1–30 minutes, and then subside. The patient feels as if he will actually die or go crazy. We are not talking about uneasiness; we are talking about full-blown panic. The person may continue to feel nervous or upset for several hours, but the attack itself lasts only a matter of minutes. If a patient says, "I've had a continuous panic attack for the past three days," he may be having intense anxiety symptoms, but not a true panic attack. In other anxiety disorders, anxiety symptoms can be very unpleasant, but are much less intense; they also can be prolonged or generalized (i.e., present most of the day and last from days to years). The distinction between "symptoms" and "attacks" is very important when it comes to treatment. Please refer to Figure 18.

The six anxiety syndromes can be distinguished by the following characteristics:

1. *Generalized Anxiety Disorder.* The key here is *long-term,* low level, fairly continuous anxiety. Patients with this disorder *may* have no specific current life stressors. To them, daily living provokes anxiety. Such people are chronic

---

[1]Note: Obsessive-Compulsive disorder and Post-traumatic stress disorder are discussed in Chapter 6. Discussing these as separate disorders is in keeping with the DSM-5 (2013).

## Figure 18

### SYMPTOMS OF ANXIETY

- Trembling, feeling shaky, restlessness, muscle tension
- Shortness of breath, smothering sensation
- Tachycardia (rapid heartbeat)
- Sweating and cold hands and feet
- Lightheadedness and dizziness
- Paresthesias (tingling of the skin)
- Diarrhea and/or frequent urination
- Feelings of unreality (derealization)
- Initial insomnia (difficulty falling asleep)
- Impaired attention and concentration
- Nervousness, edginess, or tension

worriers, always "what-if-ing" (e.g., "What if I get fired?" "What if my check bounces?" "What if my wife leaves me?").

2. *Stress-related Anxiety.* The patient with this disorder typically functions well. However, the anxiety symptoms have recently emerged in the face of major life stresses (e.g., a serious family illness, a marital separation, etc.).

3. *Panic Disorder.* This is characterized by repeated episodes of full-blown panic, as described in the discussion of panic attacks. Often phobias will also develop.

4. *Social Anxiety.* Anxiety is experienced only when the person is in social/inter-personal settings, e.g., public speaking, asking someone out for a date, social gatherings.

5. *Medical Illnesses, and Medications Presenting with Anxiety Symptoms.* Certain diseases/conditions can at times result in biochemical changes that produce anxiety symptoms. If someone complains of nervousness or anxiety, it should never be assumed that it is simply an emotional disorder until medical causes have been ruled out (Figure 19). Likewise, a number of medications and over-the-counter products can cause pronounced anxiety symptoms (Figure 20).

6. *Anxiety as a Part of a Primary Mental Disorder.* Anxiety frequently accompanies many mental disorders (e.g., depression, schizophrenia, organic brain syndromes, substance abuse).

*Figure 19*

## COMMON DISORDERS THAT MAY CAUSE ANXIETY

- Adrenal tumor
- Alcoholism
- Angina pectoris
- Cardiac arrhythmia
- CNS degenerative diseases
- Cushing's disease
- Coronary insufficiency
- Delirium[1]

- Hypoglycemia
- Hyperthyroidism
- Meniere's disease (early stages)
- Mitral valve prolapse[2]
- Parathyroid disease
- Partial-complex seizures
- Post-concussion syndrome
- Premenstrual syndrome

[1]Delirium can occur as a result of many toxic/metabolic conditions and often produces anxiety and agitation.
[2]The mitral valve prolapse probably does not cause anxiety, but it has been found that MVP and anxiety disorders often coexist. This may be due to some underlying common genetic factor.

*Figure 20*

## DRUGS THAT MAY CAUSE ANXIETY

- Amphetamines
- Appetite suppressants
- Asthma medications
- Caffeine/energy drinks
- CNS depressants (withdrawal)
- Cocaine
- Nasal decongestants
- Steroids
- Stimulants

# ANTIANXIETY MEDICATION* TREATMENT

## When Do You Prescribe Antianxiety Medications?

Treatment differs depending on the diagnosis, so each disorder will be addressed separately.

1. *Generalized Anxiety Disorder (G.A.D.).* Many physicians have tried to treat this disorder with benzodiazepines. This presents two problems: (1) Benzodiazepines

*Also referred to as minor tranquilizers, anxiolytics, and benzodiazepines. These terms will be used interchangeably.

can cause depression in some individuals, (2) patients can develop tolerance/ dependence problems with chronic benzodiazepine use. Many clinicians think that G.A.D. is primarily a psychological (not biological) disorder and recommend psychotherapy. However, SSRIs, venlafaxine and buspirone hydrochloride, have been shown to be effective in treating G.A.D. An added feature of these medications is that patients do not develop dependence or tolerance.

2. *Stress-related anxiety.* Minor tranquilizers are very helpful in reducing anxiety symptoms (especially insomnia and restlessness) which accompany acute situational stress. The most important issue to consider is whether or not the stress is acute and likely to be of short duration. Antianxiety medications should only be used for a period of 1–4 weeks. If it is clear that this is just one in a series of chronic life crises, it is probably best not to prescribe benzodiazepines.

3. *Panic disorder.* One isolated panic attack is generally insufficient evidence of true panic disorder. However, four or more true attacks within a period of one month suggest panic disorder. Look for spontaneous attacks (most "come out of the blue") and episodes that last a matter of minutes (not hours or days). Many patients with other types of disorders say they have panic attacks but on close inspection, many do not.

4. *Social phobias.* Generally, social phobias are not treated medically but with psychotherapy and behavioral approaches. In some cases beta blockers, MAO inhibitors, venlafaxine or SSRIs have been helpful.

5. *Medical illnesses/medications causing anxiety symptoms.* In almost all instances, the treatment of choice is to treat the primary medical illness or to discontinue the offending drug. Be cautious in stopping certain drugs; for instance, if a patient stops drinking coffee abruptly, he may have significant withdrawal symptoms which mimic anxiety. Such drugs must be gradually withdrawn.

6. *Anxiety symptoms as a part of another primary mental disorder.* Treat the primary disorder. Minor tranquilizers are usually not indicated.

## Choosing a Medication

Antianxiety medications fall into five groups (see Figure 21). The primary choice of medication is based on the diagnosis. Secondarily, one should consider certain problematic side effects such as sedation and rapidity of absorption (rapid absorption may be associated with a euphoric "rush").

## Prescribing Treatment

1. *Generalized Anxiety Disorder.* There are several options, including buspirone. Unlike the benzodiazepines, buspirone is slow acting. It often requires 2–6 weeks of treatment before symptomatic improvement. The major problem encountered

with this medication is premature discontinuation by the patient. Patients often expect quick results from medications. It is important to educate the patient about onset of action. Buspirone can be effective in treating many symptoms of G.A.D., but it does not seem to decrease panic attacks. Buspirone must be taken every day; it is not a medication that is taken only when the patient feels anxious. SSRIs or venlafaxine may also be beneficial in treating G.A.D. Pregabalin is approved for treating generalized anxiety in Europe, but not yet in the United States. It may also be an option for G.A.D. Again, treatment requires 2–6 weeks before signs of symptomatic improvement emerge. If patients fail to respond to buspirone, venlafaxine, or SSRIs, if symptoms are severe, and if there is no history of alcohol or other substance abuse, benzodiazepines can be used to treat G.A.D.

2. *Stress-Related Anxiety.* All benzodiazepines are effective in treating acute stress-induced anxiety. (See Figure 21). The most important considerations in choosing a medication have to do with side effects and medication half life. The most common side effect is sedation. Intense restlessness or agitation may require a more sedating drug; however, in most instances it is better to use low sedation benzodiazepines to reduce daytime anxiety. Of course many anxious patients will present with a sleep disturbance. Insomnia will be addressed below. A second side effect is the so-called euphoric "rush" secondary to the peak in blood level of medication. Such a peak creates a good deal of sedation and can be useful if the goal is to induce sleep, but the euphoric experience can lead to abuse. In addiction-prone individuals it is best to choose a drug that avoids or minimizes this effect. Finally the half life of a medication is an important variable when it comes to discontinuing the drug (see below). Those medications listed that have a shorter half life may need to be discontinued *very* gradually so as to avoid withdrawal symptoms.

Dosage ranges vary widely as seen in Figure 21. However, a typical starting dose of lorazepam, for instance, is 0.5 mg. b.i.d. or t.i.d. Such a dose should be increased every three days as needed until a final range of 2–6 mg./day is achieved. The goal is to provide some symptomatic relief over a period of from 1–4 weeks. Should a person still experience significant anxiety after this period of time, a reassessment of the diagnosis and referral to a psychotherapist is in order.

It has long been held that long-term use of benzodiazepines is contraindicated. Although this is often true, it is not always the case. Investigations into chronic benzodiazepine use have shed new light on this clinical practice. At times patients will continue to derive benefit from long-term treatment with benzodiazepines. The key is to monitor closely for signs of increasing dosage, especially as the patient may be increasing dosage without medical advice. If in doubt, don't hesitate to get a blood level and to share your concerns openly with the patient. Addiction to benzodiazepines that arise in the course of the treatment of anxiety should be treated for what it is: an occasional and serious side effect. *Always* discontinue benzodiazepines gradually (e.g., if the patient takes 1.5 mg. of alprazolam, q.d., then each week the daily dose should be reduced by 0.25 mg. This slow taper is especially important with short half-life benzodiazepines).

## Figure 21

### ANTIANXIETY MEDICATIONS

| Disorder | Medication Generic | Medication Brand | Usual Daily Dosage Range | Rapidity of Absorption | ½ Life (Hours) |
|---|---|---|---|---|---|
| 1. G.A.D. | buspirone | BuSpar | 5–40 mg. | + | 2–8 |
| | pregabalin | Lyrica | 25–450 mg. | + | 6 |
| | SSRIs[1] | | | | |
| 2. Stress-Related Anxiety | diazepam | Valium | 5–40 mg. | +++++ | 20–50 |
| | chlordiazepoxide | Librium | 15–100 mg. | +++ | 5–30 |
| | lorazepam | Ativan | 2–6 mg. | +++ | 10–15 |
| | alprazolam | Xanax | .25–4 mg. | +++ | 6–20 |
| | hydroxyzine | Atarax, Vistaril | 10–50 mg. | + | 3 |
| | clonazepam | Klonopin | .5–4 mg. | + | 80 |
| 3. Panic Disorder | alprazolam | Xanax | .25–.8 mg. | +++ | 6–20 |
| | lorazepam | Ativan | 2–6 mg. | +++ | 10–15 |
| | clonazepam | Klonopin | .5–4 mg. | ++ | 80 |
| | antidepressants[1] | | | | |
| | MAO Inhibitors[1] | | | | |
| 4. Social Phobia | propranolol | Inderal | 20–80mg. | | |
| | SSRIs[1] | | | | |
| | venlafaxine[1] | | | | |
| | MAO Inhibitors[1] | | | | |
| 5. Stress-Related Initial Insomnia[2] | temazepam | Restoril | 15–30 mg. | +++++ | 10–20 |
| | triazolam | Halcion | .25–.5 mg. | +++++ | 2–3 |
| | zolpidem | Ambien | 5–10 mg. | ++++ | 2–3 |
| | zolidem | Intermezzo | 1.75 mg. | ++++ | 2–3 |
| | suvorexant | Belsomra | 15-40 mg. | +++++ | 1–6 |
| | doxepin | Silenor | 3-6 mg. | ++ | 15 |
| | diphenhydramine | Benadryl | 25-75 mg. | ++ | 8–10 |
| | zaleplon | Sonata | 5–10 mg. | +++++ | 1–2 |
| | eszopiclone | Lunesta | 1–3 mg. | +++++ | 6 |
| | ramelteon[4] | Rozerem | 8 mg. | +++++ | 1–3 |
| | suvorexant | Belsomra | 15-40 mg. | +++++ | 12 |
| 6. Nightmares | prazosin | Minipress | 5–20 mg. | ++ | 2–3 |

[1]See Chapter 2, Figure 5.
[2]Initial insomnia: difficulty falling asleep.
[3]non habit-forming

3. *Stress-Induced Insomnia.* Benzodiazepine sedative-hypnotics can be a safe and effective treatment for transient initial insomnia. (Recall that middle insomnia and early morning awakening are more indicative of depression and therefore should not be treated with benzodiazepines). Again, in most cases

treatment is initiated only if the insomnia is precipitated by recent environmental stress and is not a chronic problem. Chronic insomnia is extremely hard to treat. Note that the drug zolpidem tartrate is not a benzodiazepine and studies to date show that dependence is less likely with this medication. For this reason, it may be a safe alternative in individuals with a substance abuse history. Typical dosages for the various sedatives are listed in Figure 21. Other popular drugs of choice that have no addiction potential are the sedating antidepressants trazodone (dosing: 25–100 mg qhs), doxepin (3–6 mg qhs), amitriptyline (25–50mg qhs) and mirtazapine 7.5–15mg qhs).

4. *Panic Disorder.* The treatment of panic disorder has two discrete phases.

*Phase One:* Eliminate or reduce the frequency or intensity of the panic attacks with antipanic drugs. There are three main groups of antipanic drugs. Let's discuss the pros and cons of each.

   a. High potency benzodiazepines and like compounds (e.g., alprazolam, lorazepam, and clonazepam)

     *Pros.* Very effective. It works quickly. It also reduces anticipatory anxiety.

     *Cons.* Although some patients respond to low doses (0.25 mg t.i.d.), most require much larger doses (3–8 mg/day for alprazolam, 2–4 mg/day for clonazepam), and at these higher doses, sedation is a very common problem. Note: effective panic control only occurs when patients take medications on a regular 24-hour-a-day basis (i.e., *not* P.R.N.). With prolonged use, dependence will develop. *Very* gradual discontinuation is required to avoid withdrawal symptoms.

   b. Antidepressants: tricyclics, selective serotonin re-uptake inhibitors (SSRIs), venlafaxine, mirtazapine.

     *Pros.* Effective in reducing attacks. Can treat concurrent depression. Can be used for prolonged periods of time without risk of tolerance/dependence.

     *Cons.* Side effects (see Chapter 2) and delayed onset of action (2–4 weeks before symptomatic improvement). Treat in the same way and same dosage levels as you would use to treat depression. Many patients experience an initial increase in panic attacks; these are usually managed well with short term use (during the first month of treatment) of a benzodiazepine, as necessary. (Note: Bupropion is one antidepressant that apparently is not effective in treating panic attacks and may exacerbate anxiety.)

   c. MAO Inhibitors

     *Pros.* Very effective. Can treat concurrent depression. Can be used for prolonged periods of time without risk of tolerance/dependence.

     *Cons.* Delayed onset of action (2–4 weeks) and medication/dietary restrictions as outlined in Chapter 2. As with typical antidepressants, treat as you would treat depression.

*Phase Two.* Patients not only have the attacks, but develop significant anticipatory anxiety, phobias, and avoidance (a strong urge to avoid situations in which they have experienced prior panic attacks, e.g., to avoid crowded stores or driving on freeways). These problems frequently do not spontaneously remit when the panic attacks are eliminated. People continue to have intense worries that "It could happen again." Phase two involves gradual reexposure to feared situations. So, for instance, if a person is afraid of having an attack at the grocery store, he must gradually approach the feared situation. Only by repeated exposure to the situation and by a series of experiences without panic will the patient's anticipatory anxiety and avoidance diminish. The keys to successful graded reexposure are (1) to first effectively control or reduce attacks with medication and then (2) to have the patient very gradually face the phobic situation. To be effective, exposures should last for at least 60 minutes.

The duration of the underlying biochemical dysfunction is quite variable. Some people may be treated medically for six months and gradually withdrawn from medication. Others may need years of continued treatment. Like depression, the strategy with any of the antipanic drugs is to achieve symptomatic relief and then continue to treat for at least 6 months. At that point, a medication-reduction trial may be initiated. If necessary, treatment can be resumed if panic symptoms reemerge.

5. *Social Anxiety.* In most cases psychotherapy is the treatment of choice. Psychotropic medications have been used, however, in two types of social phobia. Some social phobics are extremely sensitive to rejection and this is why they are fearful of social interactions. Clinical data indicate that these patients may benefit from MAO inhibitors, venlafaxine, or SSRIs. A second type of phobia, stage fright/public speaking phobia, has been successfully treated by beta blockers such as propranolol (usually 20–40 mg., 1 hour prior to performing). Beta blockers do not eliminate the centrally mediated, subjective sense of anxiety, but do quite effectively reduce many peripheral somatic symptoms of anxiety, e.g., tachycardia, trembling.

## Common Treatment Errors to Avoid

- As noted in Chapter 2, SSRIs frequently present with increased anxiety as a side effect during the first few weeks of treatment. This is *very* problematic in the treatment of anxiety disorders and a major cause of patient-initiated discontinuation. As mentioned in Chapter 2, it is common practice to co-administer an SSRI and a minor tranquilizer during the first month of treatment (e.g., 0.25–0.5 mg lorazepam, bid or tid). For those with a substance abuse history, tranquilizers should not be used. The antihistamine hydroxyzine (Atarax; Vistaril: 10–50 mg) is a safe alternative. Generally, SSRIs begin to significantly reduce anxiety by week four of treatment, and at this time the tranquilizer can be discontinued.
- Prescribing benzodiazepines to a patient with a personal or family history of substance abuse (high risk of abusing the benzodiazepine). Watch for patient requests for higher and higher doses. In those with a history of or high risk for substance abuse there are four commonly used, non-habit-forming alternatives: trazodone (50–75 mg qhs for sleep), buspirone for generalized anxiety disorder,

mirtazapine (7.5–15 mg qhs for sleep), hydroxyzine: Vistaril, Atarax, and gabapentin (300–2400 mg qd) for generalized or stress-related anxiety.

- "Cold turkey" discontinuation or rapid taper of benzodiazepines (can result in significant withdrawal symptoms. 1–3 month gradual taper advised).
- Misdiagnosis: failure to recognize depression or an emerging psychotic illness and treating with benzodiazepines (can worsen depression and fail to treat psychosis).
- Over-sedation with benzodiazepines in the treatment of day-time anxiety.
- Benzodiazepines in treating elderly patients can cause cognitive impairment and contribute to unsteady gait and falls. Use with caution.
- Patients with anxiety disorders should consume *no* caffeine and partial responses or break-through symptoms are often due to unreported caffeine use.

## *IN EVERY CASE, REMEMBER*

Some degree of stress and anxiety is a common part of normal, daily living. Medication treatment should only be initiated if symptoms are significantly intense and severely interfere with normal functioning.

When you prescribe any kind of medication to control anxiety, it is essential to discuss the following key points with the patient:

## KEY POINTS TO COMMUNICATE TO PATIENTS

*All patients suffering from anxiety disorders:* Caffeine use should be zero and regular exercise is a very high yield intervention.

*Generalized Anxiety Disorder*
1. If buspirone, pregabalin, venlafaxine, or SSRIs are prescribed, you should expect that it will take from 2–6 weeks to notice symptomatic improvement. Daily doses are required. This is not a medication that you take only as needed.
2. Often medication treatment is not enough, and psychotherapy, stress management, relaxation training, regular exercise, and biofeedback are helpful adjuncts to medical treatment.

*Stress-Related Anxiety*
1. The following analogy is helpful. Pain killers can reduce suffering when you have a toothache, but at some point you must fix or pull the tooth. Likewise, minor tranquilizers do not cure people, but they temporarily reduce suffering. You must do something to alter the basic source of stress if lasting recovery is to be achieved. Minor tranquilizers are only for short-term use.
2. Do not abruptly discontinue minor tranquilizers, especially if they have been taken daily for several weeks. Cold-turkey discontinuation can result in withdrawal syndromes (many withdrawal symptoms are almost identical to symptoms of anxiety).
3. Do not drink any kind of alcohol if you are taking a minor tranquilizer.

## *Figure 22*

## DECISION TREE FOR DIAGNOSIS AND TREATMENT OF ANXIETY

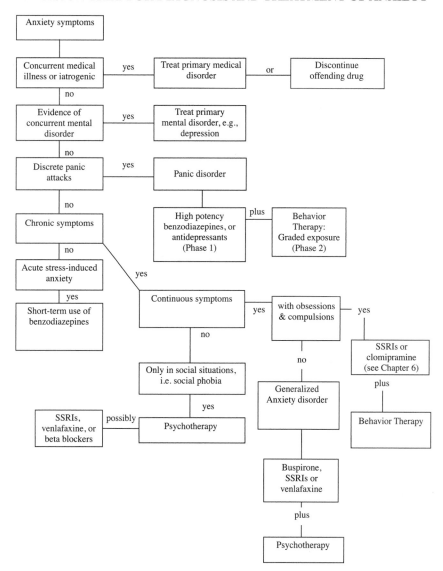

*Panic Disorder*

1. There is strong evidence that panic disorder is a biochemical dysfunction, not a psychological disorder. It can often be very successfully treated with medications.
2. Medication must be taken each day. The treatment is prophylactic and not a medication that you only take as needed.
3. The medication treats *only* the panic attacks. Once these are adequately controlled, you will need to enter Phase Two of treatment (graded reexposure) to deal with anticipatory anxiety and avoidance. In many cases this is best done with the help of a therapist familiar with behavioral techniques.
4. If MAO inhibitors are used, you must understand the dietary and medication restrictions and sign a consent form.
5. If alprazolam, lorazepam, or clonazepam are used, you must never abruptly discontinue it (medication reduction should be done gradually, generally 0.25 to 0.5 mg. per day per week).
6. If treated by antidepressants, it may take 2–4 weeks before you notice symptomatic changes.

*Social Phobias*

1. If medication is used (MAOI, SSRI, venlafaxine, or beta blockers), this must be accompanied by exposure (i.e., you must be willing to enter certain social situations and test out the water).
2. Psychotherapy is also indicated.

## Books to Recommend to Patients

1. Beckfield, D. (2004). *Master Your Panic,* Third Edition, Impact Publishers, San Luis Obispo, CA.

2. Bourne, E. (2003). *Coping with Anxiety.* New Harbinger Publications: Oakland.

3. Greist, J. H. and Jefferson, J. (2001). *Panic Disorder and Agoraphobia: A Guide,* Madison Institute of Medicine, Madison, Wisconsin.

4. Moore, B (2014) *Taking Control of Anxiety*, American Psychological Assoc., Washington, D.C.

# Chapter 5    Psychotic Disorders

## DIAGNOSIS

## Major Clinical Features and Differential Diagnosis

For practical purposes three major psychotic disorders are described: (1) schizophrenia (and schizophrenic-like disorders), (2) psychotic mood disorders, and (3) psychosis associated with neurological conditions.

Before discussing differential diagnosis, let's first briefly define *psychosis*. Psychosis is not an illness; it is a symptom associated with a number of disorders. The hallmark of psychosis is impaired reality testing (impaired ability to accurately perceive reality). The loss of contact with reality can take many forms: severe confusional states, delusions (bizarre, unrealistic thoughts), hallucinations, and marked impairment in judgement and reasoning. Having psychotic symptoms does not in itself imply a specific etiology; causes are varied. The three groups of psychotic disorders mentioned above are distinguished by the following characteristics:

1. *Schizophrenia*. Schizophrenia is generally a recurring illness; people diagnosed with schizophrenia are prone to repeated psychotic episodes. It is helpful to think about three types of schizophrenia:

   a. *Positive Symptom Schizophrenia*. This type of schizophrenia is also referred to as dopaminergic schizophrenia because of its presumed etiology: a hyperactive dopamine system. Positive systems are active, florid delusions and hallucinations; agitation and emotional dyscontrol. There are two subtypes:

      1. *Schizophreniform disorder* (Brief psychotic reaction). This disorder looks like schizophrenia but remits quicker and often does not recur.

      2. *Schizophrenia, per se.* This is a recurring or chronic disorder.

   b. *Negative Symptom Schizophrenia*. This is a neuro-developmental disorder. Negative symptoms include: flat or blunted affect, anhedonia (inability to experience pleasure), marked social aloofness/withdrawal, and the absence of florid delusions and hallucinations. Negative symptom schizophrenia tends to have an earlier and more insidious onset. As children, these people were often seen as odd and aloof.

2. *Psychotic Mood Disorders*. Both mania and depression can present with poor reality testing and other psychotic symptoms.

3. *Psychosis Associated with Neurological Conditions.* Many acute metabolic and toxic states can result in a delirium. Head injury occasionally produces transient psychotic behavior and a number of degenerative diseases (e.g., Alzheimer's) can produce periods of agitated confusion. Detailed description of psychopharmacologic treatment of various neurological conditions is beyond the scope of this book. However, it is very important to distinguish such conditions from schizophrenia and mood disorders. A brief mental status exam can be helpful. It should include a test of short-term memory, as well as tests for orientation and naming. Most neurologically based disorders that present with psychotic symptoms will also show gross impairment in recent/short-term memory; these abilities are relatively intact in schizophrenia. Damage to Wernicke's area (superior temporal lobe) can occasionally result in what looks like a schizophrenic reaction (language and thinking are grossly impaired). Wernicke's patients have a terrible time naming objects; people with schizophrenia and mood disorders do not. See the *Four Minute Neurological Exam* (in the MedMaster Series) for more hints on conducting a brief neurological exam. Figure 23 lists medical illnesses that may produce psychotic symptoms, and Figure 24 lists medications that may result in psychotic reactions.

*NOTE:* The treatment of mood disorders that present with psychotic symptoms primarily involves treating the depression (antidepressants or ECT) and adding antipsychotics to control the psychotic symptoms. Since much of this has been covered previously (Chapters 2 and 3), the focus of the following sections will be on treating schizophrenia.

### *Figure 23*

### COMMON DISEASES AND DISORDERS THAT MAY CAUSE PSYCHOSIS

- Addison's disease
- CNS infections
- CNS neoplasms
- CNS trauma
- Cushing's disease
- Delirium[1]
- Dementias[2]
- Folic acid deficiency
- Huntington's chorea
- Lewy body dementia[3]

- Multiple sclerosis
- Myxedema
- Pancreatitis
- Pellagra
- Pernicious anemia
- Porphyria
- Stroke
- Systemic lupus erythematosis
- Temporal lobe epilepsy
- Thyrotoxicosis

---

[1]Any number of toxic/metabolic states may result in delirium.
[2]Any number of dementing conditions (e.g., Alzheimer's disease) may result in psychotic symptoms.
[3]Caution: Only use quetiapine. Other antipsychotics can cause marked Parkinsonian symptoms.

*Figure 24*

## COMMON DRUGS THAT MAY CAUSE PSYCHOSIS

- Sympathomimetics (e.g., amphetamines, cocaine and "crack," a form of almost pure cocaine, many over-the-counter cold medications)
- Antiinflamatory drugs (e.g., steroids)
- Anticholinergic drugs (e.g., antiparkinsonian drugs)
- Hallucinogenic drugs (e.g., LSD)
- Marijuana
- L-Dopa (in schizophrenic patients)

*NOTE:* Older persons are often on centrally acting drugs and have less ability to tolerate their toxic effects.

## Target Symptoms

It is helpful to subdivide schizophrenic symptoms into four categories: positive symptoms, disorganization symptoms, characterological traits, and negative symptoms. (See Figure 25.)

*Figure 25*

## SCHIZOPHRENIC SYMPTOMS

### POSITIVE SYMPTOMS
- Delusions and impaired thinking
- Hallucinations
- Confusion and impaired judgment
- Severe anxiety, agitation, and emotional dyscontrol

### NEGATIVE SYMPTOMS
- Flat or blunted affect
- Poverty of thought (i.e., few or no thoughts and concrete thinking)
- Emptiness and anhedonia (no joy)
- Psychomotor retardation/inactivity
- Blunting of perception (e.g., insensitivity to pain)

### DISORGANIZATION SYMPTOMS
- Incoherent speech
- Bizarre behavior
- Extreme confusion

### CHARACTEROLOGICAL TRAITS
- Social isolation and sense of alienation
- Low self-esteem
- Social skills deficits

# ANTIPSYCHOTIC MEDICATION

## When Do You Prescribe Antipsychotic Medication?

Although many general practitioners treat anxiety and depressive disorders, most patients presenting with psychotic symptoms should be referred to a psychopharmacologist. These patients are often hard to treat. Many psychotic patients can be treated on an outpatient basis; however, hospitalization may be necessary.

Antipsychotic medications (also referred to as neuroleptics or major tranquilizers) should be started when the early signs of psychosis appear, since many times a more florid psychotic episode can be averted with appropriate early intervention.

Positive symptoms and disorganization symptoms are the primary target symptoms for treatment by antipsychotic medications. Such drugs do little to affect characterological traits or negative symptoms (with some exceptions. See page 48).

## Choosing a Medication

All antipsychotic medications are equally effective in their ability to reduce positive symptoms. The choice of medication is dictated almost exclusively by the side effect profile. For a list of antipsychotic medications, see Figure 26.

Antipsychotic medications have five primary side effects which must be taken into consideration: sedation, anticholinergic (ACH), and extrapyramidal (EPS) effects, weight gain and metabolic effects.

Before choosing a medication, assess the patient's motor state. Psychotic reactions that present with marked agitation may require more sedating drugs. Use less sedating drugs for psychoses with pronounced psychomotor retardation and withdrawal. This is a general rule of thumb, but there are exceptions.

Consider anticholinergic and EPS side effects. The most common cause for relapse is poor compliance or premature discontinuation because of unpleasant side effects. The key to successful treatment rests on how well you handle side effects.

*Extrapyramidal Side Effects.* There are four classes of EPS:

1. *Parkinson-like Side Effects.* These include muscular rigidity, flat affect (mask-like facial expression), tremor, and bradykinesia (slowed motor responses). These symptoms need to be distinguished from the flat affect and withdrawal often seen as primary symptoms of schizophrenia. Parkinson-like side effects are often diminished by the administration of anticholinergic agents (e.g., benzotropine, trihexylphenidyl, or amantadine).

2. *Akathisia.* This is an uncontrolled sense of inner restlessness. Akathisia must be distinguished from anxiety. Often, a physician may mistake it for anxiety and increase the dose of antipsychotic, only to see a worsening of the restlessness. Akathisia can be partially alleviated by anticholinergic agents. Other

## Figure 26

## ANTIPSYCHOTIC MEDICATIONS

| GENERIC | BRAND | DOSAGE RANGE[1] | SEDATION | EPS[2] | METABOLIC SIDE EFFECTS[3] | EQUIVALENCE[4] |
|---------|-------|------------------|----------|--------|---------------------------|----------------|
| _Low Potency_ | | | | | | |
| chlorpromazine | Thorazine | 50–1500 mg | High | + + | + + + + + | 100 mg |
| clozapine* | Clozaril FazaClo | 300–900 mg | High | 0 | + + + + + | 50 mg |
| quetiapine* | Seroquel[6] | 100–750 mg | High | + | + + + + | 50 mg |
| _High Potency_ | | | | | | |
| perphenazine | Trilafon | 8–60 mg | Mid | + + + + | + | 10 mg |
| haloperidol | Haldol[5] | 2–40 mg | Low | + + + + + | + + | 2 mg |
| olanzapine* | Zyprexa[6] | 5–20 mg | Mid | + | + + + + + | 2 mg |
| pimozide | Orap | 2–8 mg | Low | + + + + + | + + | 2 mg |
| risperidone* | Risperdal[5] | 2–10 mg | Low | + | + | 2 mg |
| ziprasidone* | Geodon | 60–160 mg | Low | + | + | 10 mg |
| aripiprazole* | Abilify[6] | 15–30 mg | Low | + + | 0/+ | 2 mg |
| paliperidone* | Invega | 3–12 mg | Low | + | 0/+ | 1–2 mg |
| iloperidone* | Fanapt | 12–24 mg | Mid | + | 0/+ | 1–2 mg |
| asenapine* | Saphris | 10–20 mg | Low | + | 0/+ | 1–2 mg |
| lurasidone* | Latuda | 40–80 mg | Low | + | 0/+ | 10 mg |
| brexpiprazole* | Rexulti | 1-4 | Low | + | 0/+ | 1 mg |
| cariprazine* | Vraylar[6] | 1.5-6 mg | Low | + | 0/+ | 1 mg |

[1]Usual daily oral dosage

[2]Acute: Parkinson's dystonias, akathisia. Does not reflect risk for tardive dyskinesia. All neuroleptics may cause tardive dyskinesia, except clozapine.

[3]Must monitor for blood lipids, blood glucose, and weight (BMI) at baseline, at 12 weeks and thereafter annually.

[4]Dose required to achieve efficacy of 100 mg chlorpromazine.

[5]Available in time-released IM format.

* These medications are often referred to as "atypical" antipsychotics in that they have significantly less potential for causing extrapyramidal side effects than older-generation "typical" antipsychotics. They are also referred to as Second Generation Antipsychotics (SGA).

In Europe during the past 15 years the treatment of acute schizophrenia is often different than in the United States. Rather than using aggressive dosing and short hospital stays, doses are lower. This requires longer hospital stays, but some data show better long-term outcomes (in terms of a reduction in primary psychotic symptoms, decreased re-hospitalization, as well as better social and occupational adjustment).

[6]Can also be used as adjuncts for treating major unipolar, non-psychotic depression. In the future, other new generation antipsychotics may also share this feature.

drugs, however, are often more successful. These include diphenhydramine, propranolol, or minor tranquilizers, such as lorazepam.

3. _Acute Dystonias_. These are muscle spasms and prolonged muscular contractions, usually of the head and neck. These can be resolved quickly with intramuscular anticholinergic agents, or treated prophylactically with oral anticholinergics.

4. *Tardive Dyskinesia (TD)*. TD is generally a late onset EPS. This is a very serious and often irreversible effect of antipsychotic medication treatment. It affects about one out of 25 people treated for a period of one year, and by seven years of continuous treatment, it affects one in four (in those treated with typical antipsychotics. TD rates are lower with newer, atypical drugs). Symptoms include involuntary sucking and smacking movements of the mouth and lips, and can include chorea in the trunk and extremities. Although various drugs have been used to reduce TD symptoms (e.g., baclofen, sodium valporate, lecithin, and benzodiazepines), there is no true cure. Treatment starts with stopping the medication. Initial worsening of the dyskinesia is expected, as the drug not only causes the syndrome but also tends to mask it. Be patient, for months if necessary, and TD will often remit. But control of severe psychosis usually outweighs the problem of TD. All patients receiving antipsychotics *must* sign an informed consent form which explains the risks of TD. Extrapyramidal symptoms in general, as well as tardive dyskinesia are seen less frequently in atypical antipsychotics, and not at all in the drug clozapine.

*Anticholinergic Side Effects*. Dry mouth, constipation, blurry vision, urinary hesitation, occasional delirium.

*Weight Gain*. Significant weight gain is a common problem with many of the antipsychotics (and may be a contributing factor increasing the risk of diabetes). Among the newer-generation antipsychotics two agents are recommended to avoid or minimize weight gain: ziprasidone (minimal weight gain) or aripiprazole (not associated with weight gain). It is not yet clear whether the decreased weight gain with these agents is associated with a lower risk of diabetes.

*Metabolic Symptoms*. Increased risk of hyperglycemia, type II diabetes, weight gain, and elevations of triglycerides and cholesterol have been found in new generation, atypical antipsychotics, more commonly in clozapine and olanzapine. Olanzepine and clozapine have the highest incidence of metabolic side effects. Risperidone, paliperidone, and quetiapine have a modest risk of these metabolic side effects. Thus patients treated with these drugs should be monitored carefully for these potential adverse effects. Such metabolic effects are rare in aripiprazole and ziprasidone. The newest SGAs (iloperidone, asenapine, and lurasidone) appear to have low risk for metabolic side effects, but at the time of writing this book they are considered to be new enough that only time will tell if they, in fact, are rather free from these side effects. For these reasons, treatment of psychotic disorders is often more appropriately carried out by a psychiatrist.

*Additional Side Effects*. Several potentially serious additional side affects can occur with antipsychotic medications, including agranulocytosis, possible prolongation of QTc interval (thioridazine, clozapine, mesoridazine, ziprasidone), impaired temperature regulations and thus increased risk of heat stroke or hypothermia, and neuroleptic malignant syndrome (a very rare syndrome that presents with fever, extrapyramidal rigidity, severe autonomic dysfunction and in some cases death).

## Prescribing Treatment and What to Expect

Antipsychotic medications are generally started at low to moderate doses and titrated up until there is reduction in the more disruptive aspects of the psychotic reaction, e.g., agitation. (*Note:* In the past, some clinicians have recommended "rapid neuroleptization," i.e., very high initial doses of neuroleptics. This treatment approach is controversial and not recommended.) Divided doses may be helpful initially; however, after a few days, a switch to a once-a-day bedtime dose is advisable. Dosage ranges are extremely broad and vary considerably from patient to patient. In outpatient practice, an initial starting dose might be olanzapine 2.5 mg./day or quetiapine 100 mg./day. Inpatients are often treated at higher initial doses. See Figure 26 for dosage ranges. Antipsychotic medications must be taken each day.

Symptomatic improvement initially is seen as a decrease in arousal, emotional dyscontrol, and agitation. Poor reality testing, hallucinations, and disordered thinking may take much longer to respond. In many chronic schizophrenics, these latter symptoms may take a number of weeks to respond.

Assuming a good response, how long do you continue to treat? If the psychotic episode is a first episode, the rule of thumb is to decrease to a maintenance dose and continue to treat for one year. If the episode is a repeated episode, it will probably be best to treat for two to three years before a medication-free trial is initiated. Always, owing to the risk of TD, one should treat at the lowest possible dose that provides symptomatic relief.

## KEY POINTS TO COMMUNICATE TO PATIENTS

1. It is important to describe side effects to patients, especially akathisia. This side effect can be extremely unpleasant, yet often it is not spontaneously reported by patients. If it occurs and is not treated, this will greatly increase the risk of non-compliance, as well as increasing the patient's suffering. So tell patients, "You may notice an inner feeling of restlessness or nervousness. If you do, please tell me. Do not just discontinue the medication. Most side effects can be treated."

2. Schizophrenia is a relapsing disorder and it is extremely important to keep taking medication even if things seem fine. Premature discontinuation is the primary cause of relapse.

3. The total length of treatment is likely to be at least one year and often longer for more chronic schizophrenia.

4. Antipsychotic medications are not addictive.

5. You should avoid prolonged exposure to high temperatures and sunlight (some antipsychotics have photosensitivity as a side effect).

6. Avoid amphetamines, cocaine, and L-Dopa because these drugs almost always exacerbate psychoses.

7. You and your relatives need to know about and explain the risk of tardive dyskinesia (and sign appropriate consent forms.)

*Figure 27*

## DECISION TREE FOR DIAGNOSIS AND TREATMENT
## OF PSYCHOSIS

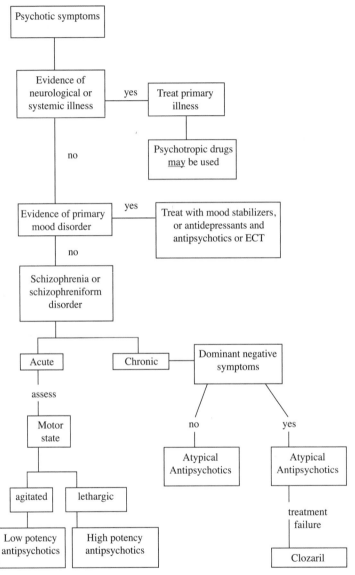

*Note:* In most cases due to favorable side effects, atypical antipsychotics are advised over
the use of typical antipsychotics (unless long-acting IM antipsychotics are warranted).

# Treatment-Resistant Schizophrenic Disorders

There are three main reasons why schizophrenic patients may not respond to antipsychotic medication:

1. *Poor compliance.* Often this is due to the unpleasant side effects. Many times patient education and proper medical management of side effects resolve the problem. Sometimes, patients simply forget to take their medication. In such cases, treatment with time-released intramuscular forms of antipsychotics can be helpful. Additionally, involving the family in treatment can significantly enhance compliance.

2. *Inadequate doses.* Blood levels can be monitored and doses increased as indicated.

3. Negative symptom schizophrenics may have a different underlying pathophysiology and often do not respond well to traditional antipsychotics. These patients are hard to treat.

Several, "atypical" antipsychotic medications have shown promise in treating the negative (as well as positive) symptoms of schizophrenia. The first is clozapine (brand name Clozaril). Clozapine became available in the United States in 1990. This medication is considered to be an atypical antipsychotic agent; its pharmacologic profile is different from other existing antipsychotics. The first important feature is that clinical trials show it to be effective in treating many schizophrenic patients who have failed to respond to standard antipsychotic drugs. This includes a number of patients that presented with negative symptoms (as well as other treatment-resistant schizophrenics). The second important and unique feature is the virtual lack of acute extrapyramidal symptoms and few reported cases of tardive dyskinesia. This medication does have two significant potential side effects: (1) The incidence of clozapine-induced agranulocytosis (a potentially fatal blood dyscrasia) is between 1 and 2%, as compared to the incidence seen in other antipsychotics (about 0.1%). This problem, however, is proving to be avoidable through a mandatory hematological monitoring program (weekly medication dispensing occurs only if the patient's white blood cell count is normal). Since implementing this program, there have been no fatalities in the 15 cases of clozapine-related agranulocytosis reported in the United States. If there is a low WBC count, medication is immediately discontinued and, to date, all such cases have been reversible. (2) A second troublesome side effect is a fairly high incidence of seizures (about 1–2% at low doses and 5% at higher doses). Despite these problematic features, clozapine appears to represent an important breakthrough in the management of otherwise treatment-resistant schizophrenic disorders.

The newest additions to the "atypical" list are aripiprazole, risperidone, olanzapine, quetiapine, paliperidone, ziprasidone, brexpiprazole, and cariprazine providing additional options for treating both positive and negative psychotic symptoms with a much more benign side effect profile when compared to standard antipsychotics. These medications do not have the high incidence of agranulocytosis seen with clozapine.

## Consequences and Outcomes of Long-term Schizophrenia

A small percentage of people suffering from schizophrenia eventually no longer exhibit active psychotic symptoms and go on to function, at least by way of maintaining employment and limited social contacts (sometimes without the use of antipsychotic medications). This generally occurs during their 40s and 50s. However, a number of people suffering from schizophrenia, at some point, no longer show positive symptoms or gross disorganization of thinking. They have moved into a phase of the illness characterized by the following:

a. Marginal personal hygiene
b. No social contacts outside of immediate family members
c. Few if any interests
d. Chronic unemployment and in general poor role functioning

These residual symptoms are rarely successfully treated by psychoactive medications.

## Common Treatment Errors to Avoid

- Akathisia (extreme inner sense of restlessness) is a very common side effect that is quite uncomfortable and a primary cause for patient-initiated discontinuation. Remarkably, many schizophrenic patients will not spontaneously complain of this side effect, but simply discontinue. It is therefore important to inquire specifically about the presence of akathisia during follow-up visits.
- Be especially watchful for early signs of tardive dyskinesia. Early signs can be elicited by having the patient lay his/her arms on lap while seated, extending the fingers in a relaxed, downward position over the knees. *Note:* Look for the presence of spontaneous, purposeless, jerking movements of the fingers.
- Antipsychotics often produce significant emotional blunting and apathy or Parkinsonian symptoms which may be mis-identified as negative symptoms (in such cases, raising the dose will likely exacerbate the side effects).

## Books to Recommend to Patients and Their Families

1. Torrey, E.F. (2006). *Surviving Schizophrenia: A Family Manual*, Harper and Row Publishers.

2. National Institute of Mental Health *Understanding Schizophrenia*. 2012.

# Chapter 6    Miscellaneous Disorders

In this chapter we would like to briefly discuss six additional disorders for which psychotropic medications can be useful.

## OBSESSIVE-COMPULSIVE DISORDER

### Major Clinical Features

The major features of this disorder are recurring obsessions (persistent, intrusive, troublesome thoughts or impulses that are recognized by the patient as senseless) and/or compulsions (repetitive behaviors or rituals enacted in response to an obsession, e.g., repeatedly checking to see if doors are locked, compulsive hand washing, or counting). In order to meet the criteria for obsessive compulsive disorder, the obsessions and/or compulsions must create significant distress or be time consuming enough to interfere with normal routines.

### Medication Treatment

Treatments of choice include the use of serotinergic antidepressants (see below) often in combination with behavior therapy. Without behavior therapy, full relapse is likely with discontinuation. Thus, chronic medication treatment is generally necessary. Where most anxiety disorders generally respond to antidepressant treatments in 4–8 weeks, often progressive and gradual improvement in obsessive compulsive symptoms continue to be seen during the first 12 months of treatment. At about a year, generally a plateau is reached.

### Figure 28

| NAME | | | | |
| Generic | Brand | Dose Range | Sedation | ACH Effects |
| --- | --- | --- | --- | --- |
| clomipramine | Anafranil | 150–300 mg | Hi | Hi |
| fluoxetine | Prozac[1] | 20–80 mg | Low | None |
| sertraline | Zoloft[1] | 50–250 mg | Low | None |
| paroxetine | Paxil[1][2] | 20–50 mg | Low | Low |
| fluvoxamine | Luvox[1] | 50–300 mg | Low | Low |
| citalopram | Celexa[1] | 10–60 mg | Low | None |
| escitalopram | Lexapro[1] | 5–20 mg | Low | None |
| vilazodone | Viibyrd[1] | 10–40 mg | low | None |

[1]Often higher doses are required to control obsessive-compulsive symptoms than the doses generally used to treat depression.
[2]Should not be used during pregnancy.

# BORDERLINE PERSONALITY DISORDER

## Major Clinical Features

Borderline personality disorders constitute a very heterogeneous group of individuals that suffer from long-term emotional instability. As a group they are characterized by the following features: a pattern of chaotic, unstable relationships, extreme neediness, significant emotional lability, impulsiveness (e.g., self-mutilation, suicide attempts, substance abuse, very poor frustration tolerance, sexual promiscuity), anger control problems (e.g., pronounced irritability, temper tantrums, etc.), a tendency to develop significant bouts of anxiety and depression, and chronic feelings of emptiness. Some borderline patients can develop transient psychotic symptoms (that usually remit within hours to days). These patients are prone to a number of major psychiatric syndromes in addition to a very stable, chronic pattern of maladaptive functioning in life.

## Medication Treatment

Although there is increasing data to suggest an underlying biologic cause in many of these patients, it is generally felt that the basic disorder is an outgrowth of significant early, maladaptive psychological development (e.g., severe child neglect). Psychotropic medications do not treat the basic personality disorder, however, medications can be used to treat particular target symptoms.

Not all borderline patients are alike, and for treatment purposes, the following subgroups can be delineated to provide guidelines for choosing medications. The subgroups are defined by the presence of a dominant symptom picture. *Note:* Investigators to date have found that minor tranquilizers generally are not indicated in the treatment of borderline personality disorder. These patients often experience an increased degree of emotional dyscontrol/disinhibition with minor tranquilizers, and are at high risk for abusing such drugs.

### Figure 29

| SUB-GROUPS | DRUGS OF CHOICE |
| --- | --- |
| 1. Impulsivity/Anger Control Problems | SSRIs; atypical antipsychotics; Omega 3 fatty acids: 1–2 grams qd |
| 2. Schizotypal (peculiar thinking, transient psychosis) | Low doses of antipsychotic medications, e.g., 2.5 mg olanzapine, 1 mg. risperidone |
| 3. Extreme sensitivity to rejection/ being alone | SSRIs atypical antipsychotics |
| 4. Emotional instability | Lithium, divalproex, atypical antipsychotics |

# ATTENTION DEFICIT HYPERACTIVITY DISORDER

Attention deficit hyperactivity disorder (ADHD) affects 5%–7% of children and 4% of adults. It is now widely held that this disorder is largely due to a neurochemical disturbance (likely involving dysregulation of dopamine genetically transmitted in the frontal cortex).

Recent longitudinal/follow-up studies indicate that as many as 66% of ADHD children continue to exhibit symptoms well into adolescence and adult life, thus suggesting that potentially 2–3% of the adult population experience ADHD symptoms. The major symptoms of ADHD are outlined in Figure 30.

### *Figure 30*

### SYMPTOMS OF ADHD

- Impulsivity, e.g. acting before thinking, quick responses, poor judgment
- Difficulties in feeling motivated
- Impaired abilities for attention and concentration; distractibility
- Difficulties organizing tasks and activities
- Restlessness and "hyperactivity"
- Impaired emotional controls
- Associated features:

    Learning disabilities

    Low self-esteem

With age and maturation 33% of ADHD kids "grow out of it" and exhibit no ongoing symptoms. The remaining 66% tend to see a gradual reduction in restlessness and "hyperactivity" although other core ADHD symptoms remain.

ADHD kids and teenagers often encounter considerable social/peer rejection and academic failure. Self-esteem problems and frank clinical depression are not uncommon. Rates of substance abuse in *un*treated ADHD adolescents are high (probably best seen as an attempt to medicate-away feelings of sadness and inadequacy).

The discussion of pharmacologic treatment of ADHD with children and young teens is beyond the scope of this book (see Preston, O'Neal, Talaga, & Moore, 2021). Older adolescent and adult ADHD clients can be very successfully treated with psychotropic medications (success rates approaching 90%).

The mainstay of pharmacologic treatment of ADHD is the use of stimulants (See Figure 31). Please note that the four fast-acting stimulants listed (methylphenidate, dexmethylphenidate, amphetamine, and dextroamphetamine) can become drugs of abuse in those predisposed to chemical dependency. Thus caution should be exercised in treating patients with a substance abuse history. (*Note:* Studies of ADHD children, adolescents and adults *without* a personal or family history of substance abuse, show no tendency to abuse these stimulant drugs.) And the abuse potential does not occur with Provigil, Nuvigil, or the antidepressants listed in Figure 31.

*Figure 31*

## MEDICATIONS USED TO TREAT ADHD[2]

| GENERIC | BRAND | DAILY DOSES |
|---|---|---|
| **Stimulants** | | |
| methylphenidate | Ritalin | 5–50 mg. |
| methylphenidate | Concerta | 18–36 mg. |
| methylphenidate | Metadate | 10–40 mg. |
| methylphenidate | Daytrana (patch) | 15–30 mg. |
| methylphenidate | Quillivant (liquid) | 10–60 mg. |
| dexmethylphenidate | Focalin | 5–40 mg. |
| dextroamphetamine | Dexedrine | 5–40 mg. |
| lisdexamfetamine | Vyvanse[1] | 30–70 mg. |
| pemoline[1] | Cylert | 37.5–112.5 mg. |
| d- and l-amphetamine | Adderall | 5–40 mg. |
| amphetamine salts | Mydayis | 12.5–50 mg. |
| amphetamine sulfate | Adzenys | 3.1–18.8 mg. |
| amphetamine salts | Evekeo | 5-40 mg. |
| modafinil | Provigil | 100–400 mg. |
| armodafanil | Nuvigil | 150–250 mg. |
| **Antidepressants** | | |
| bupropion | Wellbutrin | 150–300 mg. |
| atomoxetine | Strattera | 60–120 mg. |
| **Alpha-Adrenergic Agonists** | | |
| clonidine | Catapres, Kapvay | 0.1–0.3 mg.  bid or tid |
| guanfacine | Tenex | 0.5–3 mg.  bid or tid |
| | Intuniv | 1–4 mg./day |

[1]*Note:* Vyvanse is a pro-drug and thus is less likely to be a drug of abuse.
[2]Recent times have shown a proliferation of stimulant drugs. Those listed are the most common in use.

All stimulants (except pemoline) predictably cause initial insomnia if taken after 3 pm. Thus it is often important to use other medications to provide symptomatic control during the late afternoon and evening hours. Such alternatives include the antidepressants and alpha-adrenergic agonists listed in Figure 31. In head-to-head comparisons, stimulants have been found to have more robust effects in controlling ADHD symptoms, however these alternatives can help augment effects of stimulants or may be effective as a monotherapy. An example of combined therapy: methylphenidate and atomoxetine both given in the morning . . . the stimulant remains active until mid-afternoon while the antidepressant continues to be effective through evening hours. If alpha adrenergic agonists are prescribed, bid or tid dosing is generally required. Very rare reports of arrhythmias and sudden cardiac death have been reported. This has prompted many physicians to conduct a cardiac screening prior to treating with stimulants.

Because ADHD (in adults) is almost always a life-long condition, prolonged medication treatment is the rule rather than the exception.

# AGGRESSION

## Major Clinical Features

Marked aggression (including irritability, hostility, violence), whether chronic or episodic, is seen in a number of psychiatric and neurologic disorders, including those listed in Figure 32.

*Figure 32*

### PSYCHIATRIC DISORDERS PRESENTING WITH SYMPTOMS OF AGGRESSION

- ADD/ADHD
- Anti-Social Personality Disorder
- Borderline Personality Disorder
- Conduct Disorder
- Delirium
- Dementias
- Depression
- Explosive Disorder

- Iatrogenic, e.g. steroid use
- Mania
- Mental Retardation
- Paranoid Disorder
- Post-concussion Syndrome
- Schizophrenia
- Substance Use Disorders
- Temporal Lobe Epilepsy

In most cases, the preferred strategy is to treat the primary disorder (e.g., use of antipsychotics with schizophrenics). Beyond this, certain medication treatment options exist (See Figure 33). However, it is important to note that no single treatment for aggressive behavior has been devised that has a high rate of success. The class of medications, however, that is most commonly prescribed is atypical antipsychotics. These medications often successfully treat aggression in non-psychotic individuals. The clinician must consider side effects of all potential agents and then proceed with a systematic trial of available medications until one proves to be helpful. Regretfully, severe aggression continues to be a target symptom that is very difficult to treat.

*Figure 33*

### MEDICATION OPTIONS IN THE TREATMENT OF AGGRESSION

- Antipsychotics
- Anticonvulsants (e.g. divalproex)
- Beta blockers (e.g. propranolol)
- Buspirone

- Clonidine
- Lithium
- SSRIs

# EATING DISORDERS

Eating disorders are generally categorized as follows: bulimia (periodic binge eating following by purging) and anorexia nervosa (intense fear of becoming fat and a refusal to maintain healthy, age-appropriate body weight).

Unfortunately, anorexia nervosa, which can often be a life-threatening illness, has a poor response rate to a host of standard psychotopic medications. It has been treated experimentally with the opiate antagonist, naltrexone. Atypical antipsychotics have the best track record in reducing the delusional thinking regarding the need to lose weight. Because it is potentially a very severe disorder, a referral to a psychopharmacologist or a specialized eating disorders program is almost always warranted.

Bulimia, however, often is somewhat responsive to treatment with antidepressants (even in the absence of depressive symptoms). The clinician should treat bulimia much in the same way as he/she treats depression (i.e., with regard to dosing, length of treatment, etc.). All antidepressants lower seizure threshold and this can be especially problematic in this metabolically unstable group. Thus caution is warranted (especially if treating with immediate release bupropion). The anticonvulsant topiramate and psychostimulant lisdexamphetamine have shown to be effective in the treatment of binge eating and bulimia.

# POST-TRAUMATIC STRESS DISORDER

Post-traumatic stress disorder (P.T.S.D.) may be seen in the aftermath of recently occurring severe stressful events or can present in a chronic form which continues for many years after traumatic experiences (the latter is often seen in individuals who experienced very severe abuse as children). The symptoms of P.T.S.D. vary, and can include the following: generalized anxiety, panic attacks, depression, transient psychotic symptoms, intrusive symptoms (intense unwanted memories, flashbacks or nightmares) and states of emotional numbness.

The treatment of choice for P.T.S.D. is psychotherapy. Psychotropic medication treatment may be helpful in reducing certain target symptoms (treatments for panic and depressive symptoms follow general guidelines for these conditions). Four symptoms of P.T.S.D. warrant specific comments.

(1) Transient psychotic symptoms often respond to a *short course* of antipsychotic agents. Often, the doses required are somewhat lower than that generally required to treat schizophrenia. (2) Intrusive symptoms have been treated with a host of psychiatric medications. To date, the best outcomes are achieved with SSRI antidepressants. It should be noted that often high doses may be required (e.g. 60–80 mg fluoxetine or 200 mg. sertraline). (3) Although no specific medication targets emotional numbing, often once intrusive symptoms are diminished, there is a corresponding decrease in the frequency and intensity of numbness (and related symptoms such as dissociation, depersonalization and derealization). The antihypertensive drug, prazosin (Minipress) has been shown in experimental studies to significantly reduce nightmares. Starting doses are 1 mg HS gradually titrated up to doses between 10-15 mg HS. Low doses of prazosin have also been used successfully during the day time to

treat a range of P.T.S.D. symptoms. Again, dosing must be titrated gradually to avoid orthostasis. Eventual doses range from 1-5 mg given three times a day with larger doses at night to address nightmares.

Alpha adrenergic agonists (e.g., clonidine, 0.1–0.3 mg) and beta blockers (e.g., propranolol, 10–40 mg) have recently been used experimentally in the treatment of acute P.T.S.D. Preliminary data suggests not only positive symptomatic improvement, but also the prospect that if treatment is initiated within the first few hours to few days after exposure to traumatic stressors, it may prevent the development of more chronic forms of P.T.S.D. (a good deal of research now suggests that severe stress can result in the release of excessive amounts of glutamate and cortisol that may be neurotoxic; subsequent brain damage can contribute to acute P.T.S.D. developing into more severe, more chronic, and more treatment resistant cases of P.T.S.D. Possibly one acute action of these medications is to reduce over-activation of stress hormones and certain central neurotransmitters, and thus, in a sense, be neuro-protective).

Finally, it is important to note that although P.T.S.D. presents with prominent anxiety symptoms, treatment with benzodiazepines (minor tranquilizers) has been shown to be relatively ineffective and may actually contribute to less favorable long-term outcomes.

## Books to Recommend to Patients and Their Families

### Obsessive-Compulsive
Steketee, Gail, et al. (2006). *Obsessive Compulsive Disorder: The Latest Assessment and Treatment Strategies.* Compact Clinicals, Kansas City.

### ADHD
Barkley, Russell (2013). *Taking Charge of ADHD;* Revised Edition. Guilford Press, New York.

Carroccia, G. (2019) *Treating ADHD/ADD in Children and Adolescents.* Charles C. Thomas: Springfield, Illinois

### Borderline Personality Disorder
Kreisman, J. and Krauss, H. (2010). *I Hate You—Don't Leave Me: Understanding Borderline Personality Disorder,* Price Stern: New York.

Mason, P. and Kreger, R. (2010). *Stop Walking On Eggshells,* New Harbinger, Oakland, CA.

Preston, J. (2006) *Integrative Treatment for Borderline Personality Disorder.* New Harbinger: Oakland, CA.

### Aggression
McKay, Matthew (2000). *The Anger Control Workbook,* New Harbinger Publications, Oakland, CA.

### Eating Disorders
Costin, C. (2006). *Eating Disorders Sourcebook.* McGraw-Hill: New York.

### Post-traumatic Stress Disorder
Schiraldi, Glenn (2009). *Post Traumatic Stress Disorder Source Book,* McGraw-Hill, New York.

# Chapter 7    Over-the-Counter Medications
## and Dietary Supplements

In the United States each year people spend $500 million for over-the-counter (OTC) herbal remedies and dietary supplements that purport to treat psychiatric disorders. There are a number of reasons that many people choose these products rather than seeking more traditional medical solutions. Some of these reasons include: wanting to only use "natural" medications; fears that standard FDA-approved pharmaceuticals may be habit forming or prone to causing serious side effects; needing to find treatments that are less expensive than prescription drugs; desiring to seek relief from psychiatric symptoms without consulting a mental health professional or personal physician (this is largely about negative stigma associated with treatment for mental illnesses). Additionally, many patients seeking out psychotherapy may have already been taking such OTC drugs when they enter therapy, and many will have questions regarding the efficacy and safety of these products.

During the past two decades there has been a significant increase in the number of patients seeking complementary and alternative medicine (CAM). Recent surveys show that up to 40% of Americans have turned to CAM for the treatment of many illnesses. Mood-altering agents such as St. John's wort and SAMe are among the top selling dietary supplements. It is important to be aware that 70% of people taking these products never mention this to their physician. At times this can be very problematic  especially as this relates to drug-drug interactions.

There are several OTC products that have been shown to be effective in treating depression and anxiety. These are reviewed below (note: many OTC products have been suggested to have indications in the treatment of psychiatric disorders; we are only including those that have the strongest empirical evidence). First however, it is important to address three concerns. Many individuals prefer to be treated with something that is "natural" assuming that natural also means "safe." This is not always the case. Some OTC products are well known for producing significant (and sometimes dangerous) drug-drug interactions; most notably: St. John's Wort. This herbal product has complex effects on liver metabolism, inhibiting some liver enzymes and inducing others, thus leading to a number of potential serious drug-drug interactions.

Secondly, the FDA does not have oversight of dietary supplements. Many of these products are not quality controlled. There have been numerous cases in which some products did not contain the advertised amount of the drug or where impurities or contaminants have been found (e.g. lead, mercury, arsenic). With no standardization requirements the consumer has no way to determine if the product they buy is safe or if it contains the actual ingredient at the advertised dose/potency. Two agencies: US Pharmacopia (USP) and National Sanitation Foundation (NSF) independently evaluate OTC drugs and dietary supplements. If their insignia (USP or NSF) is printed on the bottle, the customer can be assured that the product they are buying is the real thing at the dose/potency listed on the bottle and that it is free of contaminates. These two agencies, however, do not evaluate efficacy.

A third and very important issue is that generally these products are purchased and taken without medical supervision. People self-diagnose and then take the medications/supplements. At times this can lead to a disaster. This is especially true when people have undiagnosed bipolar disorder and they begin taking St. John's Wort, 5-HTP or SAMe (all of which have been shown to reduce depressive symptoms). The person experiences significant depressive symptoms, assumes they have some type of garden variety depression and then they begin to self-treat. Within 3–5 weeks the drug can provoke switching into a manic episode. It is well known that any treatment that reduces depressive symptoms can potentially provoke manic episodes in people who have bipolar disorder. In a number of countries where there is wide spread use of herbal and dietary supplements to treat psychiatric disorders there are strong incentives for people to first be carefully diagnosed by a physician or other type of mental health professional and then be followed and monitored by a physician as the treatment begins. For example, in Germany, these products are available over-the-counter for purchase, however if the patient is evaluated and treated by a physician, they receive a prescription and the medicine at no cost (paid for by the government). Those who want to take herbal OTC drugs should be carefully evaluated and followed by a physician or mental health expert.

## Over-the-counter options for Treating Depression

Five OTC products have research support for efficacy in treating depression: St. John's Wort, SAMe, 5-HTP, Omega-3 fatty acids and folic acid. The first 3 of these have been used to treat depression as a stand-alone monotherapy. Folic acid and omega-3 fatty acids are used to augment antidepressants. Summarized below is information regarding dosing and side effects for each of these products. As side effects are discussed keep in mind that *all* of these products can provoke mania in bipolar patients.

In a meta-analysis of studies evaluating the efficacy of St. John's wort, this drug has treatment outcomes showing it to be equally effective to prescription antidepressants (Linde, K. et al. Cochrane data Base of Systematic Reviews, 2011). This drug is well tolerated with side effects including mild nausea and sometimes photosensitivity. In order to treat severe depression, the doses need to be high (i.e. 1500–1800 mg per day). Treatment should begin at 300 mg a day and over a period of 2 weeks titrate up to 1500 or 1800 mg a day. These higher doses require three times a day dosing to avoid nausea and other GI symptoms which would occur if the total dose were to be taken once a day. As noted above drug-drug interactions can be problematic and sometimes dangerous. It is best to check with a pharmacist who can review all of the patient's medications to determine if adverse interactions are likely to occur.

SAMe is a naturally occurring bio-molecule. Meta-analyses show it to be equally effective to standard antidepressants (Williams, A., et al. 2005). Most people who take SAMe have no side effects, but side effects do occur and can include: nausea, diarrhea, headaches, restlessness and insomnia. It should never be given with MAOIs. Doses required to treat severe depression need to be between 800 and 1600 mg a day.

Omega-3 fatty acids have shown promise as an augmenting agent in the treatment of depression. They are superior to placebo as an augmenting medication. There are several types of omega-3 fatty acids: linolenic acid (derived from flax seed and walnut oils), EPA and DHA (the latter two, from fish oil). A good deal of research has revealed that fatty acids from fish oil are significantly more bioavailable in the brain than that derived from nut and seed oils. Additionally, EPA is the specific omega-3 fatty acid that appears to have an impact on depression. On close inspection of the product label, many fish oil products have relatively small amounts of EPA. In the studies where omega-3 is effective in treating depression the amount of EPA required to produce positive results is 1000 mg–2000 mg (1–2 grams). Omega-3 at these doses is very well tolerated with few side effects. It can produce some mild GI upset.

5-HTP which is derived from tryptophan is an effective and well tolerated antidepressant (one used frequently in Japan). It treats major depression (Shaw, K.A., et al. 2008, Cochrane data base of systematic reviews). Typical dosing is 300 mg a day and this can be increased to 600 mg a day. At times 5-HTP can cause serotonin syndrome and should not be given along with prescription antidepressants.

Folic Acid has been shown to be an effective augmenting drug when added to antidepressants (Taylor, MJ, et al., 2003. Updated 2005, Cochrane Database of Systematic Reviews). The typical dose is 400–800 mcg per day, and at these doses there are no side effects. If a patient is being treated with Depakote, higher doses of folic acid are required because Depakote depletes folate. The recommended dose is 1 mg a day for women and 2 mg a day for males.

Some individuals lack the liver enzyme that transforms folic acid into l-methyl folate (folic acid cannot cross the blood brain barrier; l-methyl folate does). L-methyl folate is available as the prescription Deplin (7.5–15 mg) which can be used to augment the treatment of depression.

## Other OTC Products

The research data base for the following products is scant. However, the following may be options for treating certain target symptoms.

Melatonin: 0.5 to 5 mg one hour prior to sleep. It should not be used as a sleeping pill. Rather, melatonin helps to cool the body down during sleep which facilitates entry into slow wave (deep) sleep. Higher doses can cause drowsiness and also may increase depression. The lower dose strategy is recommended. Melatonin is not habit-forming and is well tolerated.

Magnesium-threonate is becoming a treatment of choice for muscle tension at night and as a non-habit-forming sleeping aid. The doses range from 500-2000 mg. It is also available in topical form for cramping in hands and feet.

Chamomile Tea: One study demonstrated that daily use of chamomile can effectively treat generalized anxiety disorder (Jun, J., et al., 2014). In the study symptomatic improvement was seen when subjects consumed between 1200–1500 mg a day. It is difficult to know how many milligrams of chamomile is found in a cup of tea, but it is estimated that a 6 ounce cup of chamomile tea contains 1200–1500 mg. Chamomile tea has no side effects.

Valerian: This has been used since the days of Hippocrates as a tranquilizer and a sedative hypnotic. Doses used to treat insomnia are 300–900 mg. The mechanism of action is not well understood, but it is hypothesized to interact with GABA/benzodiazepine receptors and *may* be habit forming in people who are prone to substance abuse.

Warning: Over-the-counter dietary supplements are not regulated by the FDA and many products do not contain the actual, advertised ingredient or may contain contaminates (most notable, high levels of mercury in fish oil products). Thus these supplements should be obtained at reputable health food stores.

# References

Jun, J., et al. (2014) Long term chamomile treatment for anxiety disorders. Journal of Clinical Trials. November: (5): 188.

Linde, K., et al. (2008, updated 2011) *St. John's wort for major depression.* Cochrane Database of Systematic Reviews. Issue 4, Art. No.: CD000448. DOI: 10. 1002/1465 1858. Pub. 3.

Shaw, K.A., et al. (2002, updated 2008) *Tryptophan and 5-HTP for depression.* Cochrane Database of Systematic reviews. Issue 1, Art. No.: CD003198. DOI 10.1002/1465 1858.

Taylor, M.J., et al. (2003, updated 2005) *Folate for depression.* Cochrane Database of Systematic Reviews. Issue 2, Art. No.: CD003390. DOI: 10. 1002/ 1465 1858.

Williams, A., et al. (2005) *SAMe as treatment for depression. A systematic review.* Clinical Investigative Medicine. June: 28(3): 132–139.

# Chapter 8  Enhancing Medication Adherence

Both in general medicine and psychiatry, the number one cause of treatment failure is not taking medications as prescribed. In numerous studies people with chronic illnesses often discontinue their medications or do not take them as prescribed (Shea, 2006). There are a number of reasons for non-adherence. Those commonly seen in patients treated with psychiatric drugs include the following:

1. Many psychotropic medications require weeks of treatment before the first signs of clinical improvement are experienced. Most psychiatric disorders (especially depression) result in patients feeling pessimistic and hopeless. Even if they have been told about the need to wait in order to see improvement, after a few days frequently patients conclude that the drug is not working. They discontinue the medication. They also may drop out of treatment all together. What makes this especially difficult to deal with is that they do not share their feelings and concerns with the treatment provider.

2. Side effects often lead to medication discontinuation. At times side effects are intense and unpleasant, and may frighten the person. A common example is when the side effect *activation* (acute onset anxiety) occurs following the first dose of an antidepressant prescribed for a person suffering from an anxiety disorder or major depression where there is agitation or co-morbid anxiety. Intense anxiety not only may lead to medication discontinuation, but also may leave the patient traumatized by the experience to the point that they decide to never seek psychiatric treatment again. This decision (especially for those with chronic mental illnesses) can lead to life-long consequences (i.e. never again seeking treatment that could potentially do a lot to reduce their suffering). Additionally, side effects such as weight gain or sexual dysfunction are the cause of patient-initiated discontinuation.

3. *Fears:* Worries about adverse medication effects such as addiction are not uncommon. Another common and very understandable fear has to do with possible increases in suicidality in those taking antidepressants. Antidepressant advertisements on television always state that increased suicidality may occur with antidepressants. One of the biggest problems is when such fears go unexpressed; patients may, for various reasons, not tell their physician. If the concerns are brought to the prescriber's attention it is generally addressed by providing information regarding risks and benefits (for example, discussing the complex issues anticipated with antidepressant treatment and possible increases in suicidality). Providing this kind of information often however is not

initially effective. What patients (and parents of children and teenagers seeking treatment) first need is to really be heard. There is a time and place to provide information about these risks, but until our patients have had a chance to truly discuss their fears, such information may fall on deaf ears.

4. *Psychological dynamics:* Here are a few of the most commonly encountered in clinical practice.

    a. Some medications have sedation or other side effects that may leave the patient feeling out of control. The experience of loss of control accompanies many psychiatric disorders. Medication side effects can, at times, exacerbate these.

    b. The perception that the prescriber sees their problem only from a biological perspective. The patient perceives that a drug may or may not help, but their personal, emotional issues are ignored.

    c. There may be *secondary gain* from continuing to be "sick". Secondary gain may be conscious but it also can be unconsciously motivated.

    d. Feeling overwhelmed, the patient cannot adequately take in and process what the doctor has told them about medication treatment and what to expect from this treatment. Many people leave an appointment with their primary care doctor and begin to take antidepressants. The prescriber may have done a good job informing the patient about the fact that antidepressants often require 2-4 weeks before they begin working. Depressed persons often have difficulty with memory owing to decreased capacity for maintaining attention and concentration. After 3 days of taking their medicine, they notice no signs of improvement and forget the information the doctor provided. They conclude the antidepressants don't work and discontinue.

    e. Negative stigma regarding mental illnesses certainly still persists. Taking a medication is a concrete reminder that "I have a psychiatric disorder." This is a significant issue and can lead to non-adherence.

    f. Finally, messages from close friends and family may undermine treatment. For example, "Hey man, I heard that that drug can make you suicidal" or "You don't need medicines; if you just try harder you can pull yourself out of this" or "People get addicted to these drugs. I wouldn't take it." In *some* 12-step programs there is pressure put on members to stay away from all "mind altering" drugs. Certainly some classes of drugs do pose real dangers of addiction in those vulnerable to substance abuse (e.g. minor tranquilizers), however most classes of psychiatric drugs are not addictive. The impact of these social and interpersonal pressures can be substantial.

All of these reasons for non-adherence should be kept in mind, especially when the patient isn't getting better. According to psychiatrist Shawn Shea, patients always weigh the pros and cons of medication they are taking. This often is done in a non-systematic way and the decision "to take or not to take" is not shared with their doctor. It is always important to bring up the topic in a preemptive way, at the time the prescription is first written (Shea, 2006):

1. Consider the pros and cons: effectiveness of the drug, side effects, and any psychological issues as discussed above.

2. Anticipate side effects: share with the patient, "I'm sure you know that some medications have side effects, and you may experience this. It matters a lot to me to make sure this therapy is effective, so please don't hesitate to tell me if you encounter any side effects. If you do, we'll find a way to deal with it." The weighing of pros and cons is best done in the therapist's office where things can be systematically evaluated by both the patient and the clinician.

3. Periodically ask the patient for an assessment of their medication: "How well would you say you are doing on the medicine?"

4. Inquire about what family members are saying about the patient's medical treatment.

When side effects do emerge it is important to evaluate how severe they are. Are they tolerable? Are they disabling or interfering with important life activities? Might the side effects diminish with time?

An important key to good treatment outcomes is to give patients (and parents) time to really explore any concerns or worries that they might have about the psychiatric medication being recommended. For instance, a patient may express fears of addiction if they take an antidepressant. As noted above, just giving them information about the drug being non-addictive often is not effective. It is considerably more helpful to explore in some detail with the patient how they feel about it and what they have been told about the drug. Truly hearing the patient's concerns is, first and foremost, a decent way to interact with a fellow human being. It also may flesh out worries that have gone unspoken. This kind of thoughtful way to address fears and worries not only helps reduce non-adherence, but it can also contribute to establishing a positive therapeutic alliance. For a more in-depth discussion of medication adherence issues please refer to the excellent book by Shawn Shea (2006).

*Note:* Parts of this chapter are adapted from: Preston, J.D., O'Neal, J.H., Talaga, M. & Moore, B.A. (2021). *Handbook of Clinical Psychopharmacology for Therapists* (Ninth Edition). New Harbinger: Oakland.

# Chapter 9 Non-Response and "Breakthrough Symptoms" Algorithms

When the diagnosis is made and treatment initiated, if there is a failure to respond to treatment, then the following algorithm can provide a strategy for re-evaluation:

## NON-RESPONSE CHECKLIST

1. Re-evaluate the initial diagnosis

2. Rule out co-existing medical illness

3. Rule out substance abuse (which often interferes with the metabolism of psychotropic medications and/or exacerbates psychiatric symptoms)

4. Rule out medication-induced psychiatric symptoms (e.g., antihypertensives causing depression)

5. Has there been an adequate trial? This always assumes:

    a. Adequate dose (may necessitate monitoring blood levels)

    b. Adequate duration of time (remember, most psychotropics require several weeks of treatment before the onset of symptom reduction)

    c. Compliance (notoriously poor among psychiatric patients). Monitor side effects.

6. Rule out drug-drug interactions that may affect pharmacokinetics

7. Psychological and psychosocial issues are not being adequately addressed (refer for psychotherapy)

8. The patient may be on the wrong class of medications and/or require augmentation.

Not infrequently a patient has a positive initial response to treatment and later experiences a return of symptoms. In such instances the clinician can assess the following:

# UNEXPLAINED RELAPSE CHECKLIST

1. Recent onset or increase in substance use/abuse

2. Sleep disturbance has become more pronounced due to increased stress, physical pain, and/or substance use (e.g., caffeine). Sleep deprivation *always* increases psychiatric symptoms.

3. Failure to comply with medication treatment

4. Significant increases in psychosocial stressors

5. Changes in underlying metabolic factors and/or neurobiologic changes (e.g. impaired hepatic or renal functioning, recent head injury, menopause)

6. Tolerance for the psychotropic medication may have developed (although this is rare).

7. Rule out an underlying medical disorder.

# Chapter 10    Case Examples

In this chapter we will present a number of case examples which illustrate commonly encountered clinical issues and problems (with suggested solutions and strategies). Although general principles are helpful in initiating treatment, in a real sense each case is unique and somewhat of an experiment. Accurate diagnostic assessment and a review of the patient's personal and health status (e.g., age, medical problems, prescription drugs being taken, etc.) will certainly help determine initial psychotropic medication choices. However, beyond this starting point, the clinician must track patient response closely to monitor for compliance, side effect problems and eventual symptomatic improvement.

In managed care, HMO, and family practice settings, compliance problems abound. This is due to five common factors: a) inadequate patient education regarding the medication, b) the emergence of side effects and c) the frequent problems of demoralization and feelings of hopelessness (i.e., many psychiatric patients come to the clinician in a state of despair and pessimism. When psychiatric medications do not rapidly provide symptom improvement or unpleasant side effects occur, many patients abruptly stop taking medications or drop out of treatment), d) inadequate follow-up, and e) general aversion to/fear of taking medications, especially psychiatric medications, for a variety of psychosocially and philosophically based reasons, which the patient often will not reveal spontaneously. Frequently such patients deteriorate and re-emerge later either in a more severe psychological state, or are seen and treated for a host of stress-related somatic symptoms.

It is our opinion that more time spent initially in diagnosis and treatment followup can contribute significantly to successful treatment outcomes. Hopefully this chapter will highlight common treatment complications and suggested action strategies.

In the treatment of anxiety and depressive disorders, the "rule of threes" seems to apply. About one-third of patients are fairly uncomplicated and can be treated successfully with psychotropic medications, brief supportive counseling and the support offered by social networks (family, friends, churches, support groups). A second third of patients are more challenging. These people experience medication-related problems (e.g., side effect problems, inadequate response to standard regimens or failure to respond to first-line medications) and/or are in need of more intensive psychotherapy where treatment by a professional therapist is indicated. Yet despite these added challenges, this group can generally be managed quite success-

---

*Note: In the United States, family practice and other non-psychiatric physicians treat the majority of people seeking help for depressive and anxiety disorders, writing 69% of all prescription for antidepressants and 90% of all prescriptions for antianxiety medications.

fully.* The remaining third are significantly more difficult to treat, have complex comorbidity, and most often must have medications managed by a psychiatrist as well as being involved in psychotherapy.

The treatment of bipolar and psychotic disorders is considerably more difficult owing to three factors: a) these severe mental illnesses often require inpatient treatment, b) the medications used can have more problematic and serious side effects (often requiring more monitoring of the patient's medical status) and c) the medication regimen often is more complicated. For these reasons, although some relatively uncomplicated and treatment-responsive bipolar and psychotic patients can be and are treated in primary care settings, a referral to a psychiatrist is usually necessary.

## CASE A: A Case of Major Depression

*Background and Presenting Problems:* Mr. E. is a 62-year-old retired draftsman. He has suffered for 20+ years from rather severe arthritis. He takes over-the-counter pain medication and currently is on no prescribed medication. Beyond the arthritis, Mr. E. is in good health. Characterologically, he can be seen as a rigid, obsessional man who has had few close friends aside from business colleagues and his wife of 35 years. He is a stamp collector and since his retirement two years ago, he has become progressively isolated and withdrawn.

Mr. E. comes to you complaining of problems with his "nerves" and insomnia. His grooming is adequate, but he appears to be quite fatigued. He reports that problems have developed over the past three months ever since his wife confessed to having a "one-night fling" with an old boyfriend while she was visiting relatives out of town. She promises that the affair is not on-going, but he worries almost constantly about her "leaving me" and harbors significant anger towards her.

Mr. E.'s symptoms include: irritability, an almost total loss of the capacity for experiencing pleasure, fatigue, an inner sense of restlessness, a 15-pound weight loss over the past three months, suicidal ideas, loss of libido and a sleep disturbance (restless sleep almost every night and early-morning awakening 5 nights out of 7 during the past six weeks).

*Diagnosis Issues:* The initial impressions are that Mr. E. has a major depression. (Because of no previous episodes of depression or mania, it is considered to be a single-episode, unipolar depression.) Although clearly this depression is "reactive" (i.e., in response to a significant psychosocial stressor), the symptom picture reveals the presence of physiological symptoms (see Figure 4) which suggest a neurochemical dysregulation and indicate that he is a candidate for antidepressants.

*Initial Medication Treatment Issues and Decisions:* Although Mr. E. is quite fatigued and yet also very anxious, you choose fluoxetine. Mr. E. is prescribed a 10 mg. q.d. dose, is given proper patient education underscoring two points: a) the medication will take 2–4 weeks to begin to yield symptomatic improvement and he needs to be patient and take the medicine as prescribed, and b) be sure to call if he notices any significant side effects. (He is told the most common side effects which may occur with this medication.) After one week on fluoxetine, you increase the dose to 20 mg. q.d. Two days later, Mr. E. Calls to say that he is feeling "jittery." You instruct him to reduce the dose to 10 mg. q.d. for a week (an alternative is to co-administer a benzodiazepine, e.g. lorazepam, 0.25–0.5 bid for three weeks). You ask him to touch base with you by phone in the next day or so. Upon follow-up, the jitteriness has disappeared and he reports no other side effects. After a week on 10 mg. q.d., he is instructed again to increase to 20 mg. q.d.; he does so this time without noticeable side effects.

*Points to Underscore:*
- Minor side effect problems are common with all antidepressants, and most can be managed by dosage adjustment. As patients tolerate lower doses, the doctor can then gradually titrate the dose up into the therapeutic range.
- Patient education and close doctor-patient communication are the keys to initiating treatment dealing with early emergent problems.

*Course of Treatment:* Let's consider three possible outcomes.

*Scenario One:* By day 18 of treatment, now on 20 mg. q.d. for nine days, Mr. E. *begins* to report less daytime fatigue, somewhat better sleep and reduced irritability. He continues on the same dose, and by day 40 almost all major depressive symptoms have resolved. He still has on-going issues with his wife (for which they are in couples counseling with their minister), but core depressive symptoms are resolved. You instruct Mr. E. to continue on the antidepressant at the same dose for an additional six months before discontinuing (a highly recommended strategy to reduce the likelihood of acute relapse). The medication is discontinued six months later and he remains asymptomatic.

*Scenario Two:* By day 30 Mr. E. reports only a slight improvement in his sleep, but otherwise remains quite depressed. At this point it is very important to ask or review a number of key questions:

- Is he taking the medication as prescribed?
- Is he abusing alcohol or illicit drugs? (Concurrent and often unreported alcohol abuse is a *very common* reason for inadequate response to antidepressants.)
- Have psychosocial stressors increased?
- Although he reported that, aside from arthritis, his general health status was good, could there be an undiagnosed medical condition contributing to his depressive symptoms (e.g., thyroid disease)? An old saying is "Dogs can have fleas *and* ticks"; always consider the possibility of symptoms related to life stressors *and* coexisting medical conditions.

If all questions have been addressed and none of these factors appear to be contributing to his lack of response, the next step will be to increase the medication dose (if and only if Mr. E. tolerates side effects).

In this scenario we will assume that he does tolerate an increase to 30 mg. q.d. of fluoxetine. After seven days on the new dose, he begins to respond positively.

Within a few weeks, all depressive symptoms resolve. He is then maintained on the *same* 30 mg. q.d. dose for six months before discontinuation.

*Scenario Three:* As above, after an increase to 30 mg. q.d., Mr. E. fails to show clinical improvement. He is maintained on the dose for two weeks. You decide to increase again to 40 mg., but after two weeks there is still little improvement. At this point there are two options: a) augment or b) switch to a different class of medication.

*Scenario Three - A:* You decide to add lithium 300 mg. b.i.d to the fluoxetine, and within two weeks, Mr. E. begins to show the first signs of symptomatic improvement. (Look for positive effects of any augmentation to occur in 2–28 days.)

*Scenario Three - B:* Mr. E. either cannot tolerate lithium or fails the augmentation trial. You decide to switch to another class of antidepressant. Thus you decide to switch to bupropion. (Since fluoxetine is a serotonergic drug, the most reasonable choice for second-line treatment is an antidepressant that affects norepinephrine.) You allow for a one week no-drug wash-out and then start bupropion, SR, beginning with a low dose, 100 mg. q.d.

In order to avoid or minimize initial side effect problems, it is advisable to start with low doses, gradually titrating up every 4–7 days, as tolerated by the patient.

The dose of bupropion is gradually increased during the first week until it reaches the therapeutic range (i.e., 150 mg) (*Note:* Since Mr. E. is 62 years old, general metabolic activity, as with most older people, is slowed in the liver, and thus may benefit from lower doses, e.g., 100 mg. q.d. However, almost without exception, younger and middle-aged adults require doses within the therapeutic range (see figure 5). As doses are increased, the clinician always monitors two variables: signs of clinical improvement and side effects. In the scenario, Mr. E. was able to reach a dose of 150 mg. of bupropion by day 7, tolerating the medication well. By day 14 he began to respond.

Had he failed the 150 mg. trial, several options still exist:

- Progressively increase the dose of bupropion up to a maximum of 300 mg. q.d. (if necessary and if tolerated).
- Take a bupropion blood level to assure that it is within the therapeutic range.
- Augment with lithium.
- Switch classes of medications to either an MAO inhibitor (after an appropriate 2-week wash-out of bupropion) or the antidepressant, venlafaxine.
- Electroconvulsive therapy is a final option if all other treatments fail and/or if his condition deteriorates and suicidal impulses intensify.

Throughout treatment the clinician should continue to monitor for the presence of alcohol use/abuse, medical problems, and the use of other prescription drugs. And it is *always* important to consider psychotherapy as an important aspect of treatment, especially in cases such as that of Mr. E., where psychosocial and interpersonal issues play such an important role in the genesis of his depression.

# CASE B: A Case of Bipolar Illness

*Background and Presenting Problems:* Mr. M. is a 20-year-old college student brought to you by his parents after a two-week history of marked change in his usual behavior. At first, he began staying up later and getting up earlier. Although his parents assumed he was studying for his impending final examinations, they were puzzled by his high energy and enthusiasm in the morning since he was usually a slow starter, especially if he did not get a good night's sleep. Concern began when they discovered that he was not, in fact, studying at all, but was working on a new computer program that would make him a millionaire. He was vague on details and brushed aside objections that he had little knowledge of computer equipment and became irritable and demanding when they questioned the wisdom and reality of this behavior. He had always been a reasonable and somewhat conservative individual. In addition, he seemed to talk incessantly and without any interest in input from others, although attempted input by others would often send him off on a tangential line of discourse. Concern turned to alarm, anger and embarrassment when he made inappropriate sexual comments to one of his mother's friends who had come to visit. The patient came for a consultation only with the firm insistence of his parents, and only to make them happy since he felt nothing was wrong with his behavior.

A history confirms the patient's prior apparent excellent pre-clinical adjustment and a negative recent physical exam and full chemistry screen prior to his tryout for a baseball team.

The patient denies drug use, and his parents had found no evidence of drug use. A urine screen for drugs of abuse is obtained and confirms no drugs.

An uncle had had several episodes of erratic and irresponsible behavior, leading to financial problems and divorce, but he was the black sheep of the family and was a heavy abuser of alcohol, which the family had blamed for his misfortunes.

*Diagnosis Issues:* At this point the prescriber should remind himself or herself of the following points:

- The diagnosis of manic states is relatively easy as it is dramatic and unlikely to be confused with other conditions *provided* drug abuse is ruled out, especially stimulants.
- Bipolar disorder is often complicated in its long-term course by associated difficulties, especially of a psychosocial nature, and drug regimens for certain variant forms of the illness. It is, therefore, usually best left to the care of a psychiatrist. This is especially true if the illness has been present for some time, is rapidly cycling, or if the patient is on other medications.
- The difficulty in treating manic or hypomanic states at the outset is usually in enlisting cooperation and compliance with treatment. A good rapport or relationship with the patient is critical; working with and through the family is often critical as well.
- Do not be misled by the ability of patients to hold it together for a doctor's visit. Those patients who are clearly manic and who exhibit the classic signs on mental status exams should be referred immediately to a psychiatrist,

except for those rare patients with insight and who present themselves for treatment (and these usually have a history of prior episodes).

- Lithium carbonate is typically the drug of choice. Failure of the patient to respond to lithium should trigger a referral to, or consultation with, a psychiatrist.

*Initial Medication Treatment Issues and Decisions:* In this case, you are fortunate in that the patient has seen you in the past for physical exams and minor medical problems, and you have had good rapport. With professional concern and authoritative directness, but without condescension, you tell the patient that while he may not agree, it is your medical opinion that he has a medical condition that is well known and produces the kind of symptoms he has been having. You may want to review the reported behavior and your own observations if they have included hypomanic or manic behavior. Do not do this in an exhortatory way but in an analytical manner which arrives at your recommendation for treatment. You then educate the patient about the major side effects of lithium and get an informed consent. If the patient attempts to minimize or escape by declaring "he'll think about it," recognize with him that you cannot make him take the medication, of course, but that you really think it is important for him to take the lithium, and proffer the prescription.

Assuming compliance, you begin lithium 300 mgs. b.i.d., with meals and measure the serum lithium level in two days on a stat basis. If the lithium level is below 1.0 meq/L, increase to 300 mg. t.i.d., and again measure the serum lithium level in two days. At each visit inquire about side effects and reassure him, if they are in a tolerable range, that they are not dangerous and will lessen in the near future. The maintenance goal is 1.0 meq/L but side effects may necessitate a compromise. Levels below 0.5 meq/L are generally considered subtherapeutic. Continue to raise the dose by 300 mg. q.d., and measure the lithium level every two days until it is 1.0 meq/L. If the patient fails to respond within two weeks, consult a psychiatrist.

*Course of Treatment:* If the patient responds beautifully, he should remain on maintenance therapy indefinitely. A patient will rarely comply with this but monthly checks over the next several months encourage the patient to share with you his feelings about having a chronic mental disorder and the need to have chronic treatment; answer those questions you can. As long as the patient remains in treatment, he will need periodic blood tests for lithium, TSH (lithium occasionally produces hypothyroidism, a serious problem when untreated but easily treated) and creatinine (lithium is excreted by the kidney, and decreased renal clearance could lead to lithium toxicity). This should be done usually about every three months. In general, proceed as in case C.

## CASE C: Another Case of Bipolar Disorder

A 45-year-old married housewife with a history of three episodes of mania and two mild depressions during her twenties presents with a request to continue her lithium and to get "blood checks." She has been quite stable on lithium since beginning treatment around the age of 28, experiencing only two mild elated periods. She is in good health except for diabetes mellitus, controlled with diet alone. The patient has been quite compliant with treatment and states that her husband is fully informed of her condition and is able to identify her mood swings, often before she does. A review of her prior medical records indicates the presence of clear criteria for bipolar disorder including one brief hospitalization for the second episode of elation during which she was engaged in some sexually promiscuous behavior, which was embarrassing and quite out of character. Her depressions were significant but not associated with suicidal behavior. She had been responsive to lithium but stopped it after leaving the hospital. She quickly responded to lithium again on the third episode of elation, obviating the need for hospitalization. The records also revealed that a lithium level of 0.8meq/L controlled her symptoms adequately, but that higher levels produced some shakiness in her hands, which she found annoying. She was quite satisfied with her care, but had recently moved to the area because of her husband's transfer secondary to a promotion. The only psychiatrist in the area was not taking new patients.

Increasingly, the family practitioner will be sought out for medication maintenance by already diagnosed and regulated patients who have moved, changed insurance coverage, or whose psychiatrist has retired or moved. Once again, the history should be reviewed and only those cases which are uncomplicated (see above points to keep in mind) should be accepted.

The follow-up interval is arbitrary, but every three months is adequate in uncomplicated situations. An elevated TSH should be treated by thyroid replacement. An elevation in lithium or creatinine levels should trigger an evaluation of kidney function. Symptoms of lithium toxicity should be reviewed with the patient and her husband, with instructions to report in if these toxic symptoms are noted at any time. These brief routine visits not only establish the rapport so vital to treatment of episodes, but they also allow the practitioner to establish a baseline mental status to compare with changes produced by a mood shift. Blood for lab studies is best drawn in the morning before eating (fluids are permitted, but milk or cream should be avoided) and before the morning lithium dose. Finally, any increase in frequency of episodes, even mild ones, should trigger psychiatric consultation.

## CASE D: A Case of Acute Situational Anxiety

*Background and Presenting Problems:* Mrs. M. is a 47-year-old bank executive. She is married and has three teenage children. Her history is one of reasonably good adjustment and no episodes of prior psychiatric symptoms. Two weeks ago her husband was diagnosed with malignant melanoma. He is undergoing treatment and the prognosis is fairly positive. However, since the diagnosis Mrs. M. has experienced a considerable amount of anxiety and worry. She can hardly put her husband's illness out of her mind, and throughout the day she ruminates. Her ability to concentrate at work has become noticeably impaired. She has frequent waves of nervousness in which she trembles and experiences a mild degree of shortness of breath and tachycardia. She also reports difficulties falling asleep (requires 1½–2 hours to go to sleep, although when asleep she is able to sleep through the night). She is in good health and currently is taking no prescription medications.

*Diagnostic Issues:* Given this presentation several important questions come to mind:

- Is there any evidence that she is clinically depressed? Many patients that initially appear to have anxiety symptoms are, in fact, depressed. This differential diagnosis is important. So you question her about important symptoms such as: self-esteem, anhedonia, decreased libido, fatigue, early morning awakening, etc.
- Is she using/abusing drugs (being especially concerned with determining the amount of caffeine use)?
- Are there any undiagnosed medical problems (remember, fleas *and* ticks) e.g., hyperthyroidism?

She is sad, especially when imagining that her husband could die. However, she does not exhibit severe or entrenched symptoms of major depression. She is not abusing drugs and, in fact, is in good health. Your diagnosis is an adjustment disorder with anxiety symptoms (i.e., stress-related anxiety).

*Initial Medication Treatment Issues and Decisions:* Brief counseling or psychotherapy is the treatment of choice for this type of disorder. Medications can also be a helpful adjunct. You tell Mrs. M. that her symptoms are understandable given her life circumstances, but you also acknowledge that the impaired concentration at work and her insomnia certainly are problematic, and *short-term* medication treatment may be helpful. One very important question must be addressed prior to initiating treatment: Is there any personal or family history of alcoholism or drug abuse? If so, she should be considered *at risk* for misuse or abuse of benzodiazepines. Assuming she denies any reported history of substance abuse, she is prescribed one of the following: a) a low dose benzodiazepine for occasional daytime use (e.g., lorazepam 0.5 mg. b.i.d, prn), if the target symptoms are daytime anxiety and impaired concentration, or b) a low to moderate dose of a hypnotic (e.g., temazepam, 15 mg. q.h.s., prn) if you choose to treat the insomnia.

Mrs. M. is told that this medication is for short-term use only (probably 1–4 weeks). Should her stressors and symptoms continue beyond this point, it will probably be necessary for her to be in counseling and to be reevaluated. If she is using these medications appropriately and circumstances warrant it, continued treatment beyond 4 weeks may be indicated and helpful. You are especially alert to monitor two issues as treatment progresses:

- Many patients may not fully benefit from very low doses of benzodiazepines, and a dosage increase may be appropriate. However, overuse of medications or ongoing requests/demands for higher doses, should alert the clinician to the possibility of benzodiazepine abuse.
- Should Mrs. M. require daily use of a benzodiazepine for more than 3 or 4 weeks, the clinician must consider that dependence can develop. Tolerance generally does not develop for the antianxiety effects of benzodiazepines; however, habituation can occur neurophysiologically and can (and often does) result in withdrawal symptoms if the medication is abruptly discontinued. Thus, when you determine that it is time to discontinue, this should be done gradually. A wise approach is to take at least one month to progressively wean Mrs. M. from her antianxiety medication (if she has been on it for more than one month).

Once again, especially in cases of reactive distress, keep in mind that counseling or psychotherapy is very important, in addition to psychotropic medications, patient education, and general reassurance.

## CASE E: A Case of Panic Disorder

*Background and Presenting Problems:* Ms. B. is a 32-year-old, single vocational counselor. Although she has not had a history of major psychiatric symptoms, she did have several bouts of "nervousness," each time in response to significant life transitions. The first of these was in high school when her family moved to a new state. It was a difficult adjustment for her. She missed her old friends a lot, and for 2–3 months felt extremely anxious. She was often afraid to leave the house, although she did manage to go to school despite her distress. She also felt afraid when her parents left her at home alone for an evening. After several months, her anxiety subsided. The second episode was when she went to college. She attended a school some 200 miles away from her home town. She again felt very anxious, developed some type of undiagnosable stomach pain, and eventually dropped out. Ms. B. moved home and enrolled in a local community college, and her anxiety subsided.

After graduation from college, she secured a job with a company in her home town and has maintained fairly close contact with her parents over the years.

Six weeks ago her father suffered a heart attack. He was in critical condition for two days, but progressively recovered and currently is doing well. However, the day after his heart attack Ms. B. experienced a full-blown panic attack. This frightened her tremendously, in part because she believed that she too was having a heart attack. Her family doctor saw her later that day, diagnosed the symptoms as anxiety, reassured her and gave her a limited prescription of diazepam, 5 mg.

However, the initial attack was not an isolated episode; in the ensuing weeks she experienced approximately four attacks per week. This continued to occur even after she was reassured that her father was making a safe recovery. Most attacks were spontaneous (not associated with acute stressful precipitants). They came on rapidly (about 2 minutes from the first sign of symptoms to the height of the attack) and subsided, usually within 5–10 minutes.

Ms. B. was again seen by her physician who ran a battery of tests and concluded that aside from the panic attacks, she was in good health.

*Diagnostic Issues:* As noted in the previous case, any time anxiety is seen as a dominant symptom, it is important to rule out medical causes, including substance use/abuse. Ms. B. denied alcohol and illicit drug use, but did admit to drinking 3–4 cups of coffee and at least one diet cola per day. Caffeine rarely causes full-blown panic attacks, although it often contributes significantly to generalized anxiety and can lower the threshold for panic attacks. Thus, she was advised to gradually (over a period of 3 weeks) replace coffee and sodas with decaffeinated beverages. The gradual reduction in caffeine was done to reduce the likelihood of caffeine withdrawal (a problem frequently seen with abrupt discontinuation). In Ms. B.'s case the reduction in caffeine did reduce some generalized anxiety and improved her ability to fall asleep at night. However, the frequency of panic attacks was relatively unchanged. It is also worth noting that the prn use of 5 mg. diazepam did little to ward off her periodic attacks.

As in the last case, the clinician asked detailed questions to assess for the presence of depression. In Ms. B's case, she was beginning to feel quite discouraged and sad. She also experienced a good deal of pessimistic thinking, low self-esteem and fatigue. But other signs of a major depression were absent.

The diagnostic impression is one of panic disorder with associated mild depressive symptoms.

*Initial Medication Treatment Issues and Decisions:* The clinician decided to use a two-pronged approach: a) she was started on the antidepressant paroxetine, and b) referred to a psychotherapist who specialized in behavioral treatment. She had developed some phobias about leaving her house, and this would be the target for behavioral treatment once panic symptoms were eliminated or reduced.

*Course of Treatment:* The initial dose of paroxetine was 20 mg. q.h.s., which she tolerated well. On day 7 the dose was increased to 30 mg. q.h.s., however, the next day she experienced two panic attacks. An *increase* in anxiety and panic symptoms often occurs during the first 2–3 weeks of treatment with antidepressants. Thus, although this was a complication, it was not completely unexpected. The clinician then decided to add alprazolam 1.0 mg. t.i.d. to the 30 mg. of paroxetine (common and often successful strategy). The panic attacks subsided; Ms. B. only experienced two attacks during the next week and these were less intense than prior attacks.

The clinician continued to increase the paroxetine dose to a level of 40 mg. q.h.s. and after three weeks reduced the dose of alprazolam to 0.5 mg. t.i.d. (for one week) followed by a further reduction (0.25 mg. t.i.d.). Since the increase in paroxetine, Ms. B. has only experienced two additional minor attacks (sometimes referred to as limited symptom attacks).

By week five the alprazolam was discontinued altogether. However, the next day Ms. B. experienced her first full-blown attack in several weeks. Two questions must be asked at this point:

- Were there any new or increased psychosocial stressors?
- Did she consume alcohol or caffeine within the past day?

In Ms. B.'s case, there were no new or increased stressors, no alcohol or caffeine use, and she did take her medications as prescribed. The most likely hypothesis was the low dose of alprazolam was, in fact, instrumental in warding off panic attacks.

The clinician reinstated the alprazolam at 0.25 mg. t.i.d. and continued the paroxetine dose at 40 mg. q.h.s. No further attacks occurred during the next week. Then the alprazolam was again discontinued. Ms. B. remained stable over the next two weeks, with only one limited symptom attack. She was also told she could take one 0.25 mg. alprazolam as needed for situational anxiety (which she did 2–3 times per week over the next two months).

With panic symptoms well controlled, the behavior therapist began using graded exposure techniques with Ms. B. to help her overcome her phobia. In addition she began to explore her feelings related to her father's illness and what she identified as "my problems growing up and separating from my parents." She continued to deal with these psychological issues in psychotherapy, long after all panic and phobic symptoms disappeared.

Nine months after starting treatment, her physician initiated a gradual reduction of the paroxetine. However, five days after taking a dose of 30 mg. q.h.s., Ms. B. had another panic attack. It was necessary to resume the 40 mg. q.h.s. dose. Four months later a gradual discontinuation trial was successful.

Psychotropic medication treatment is very effective with panic disorders, but almost always requires concurrent psychotherapy and/or behavior therapy.

## CASE F: A Case of Acute Schizophrenia

*Background and Presenting Problems:* Mr. P. is a 22-year-old, unmarried janitor, who comes to the clinic complaining of "insomnia." He has been experiencing initial insomnia, restless sleep, and "bad dreams" during the past month. He is significantly overweight and has marginal personal hygiene, but otherwise is in good health. He reports some alcohol use but denies abuse of illicit drugs. He smokes three packs of cigarettes per day and drinks "a lot of coffee."

In addition to his reported problems, upon clinical evaluation you discover that he has been hearing voices over the past few weeks. The voices generally mumble unintelligible things to him, and on occasion he will hear them say, "You are a loser." He is not especially concerned about the voices, but does worry a lot about buses that pass his apartment. "The way they slow down right by my apartment is weird . . . I think they are sent there to watch me." Beyond this vague description of the activity of buses, he can offer little additional elaboration. Mr. P. also appears to be quite anxious and somewhat agitated.

Mr. P. graduated from high school with a C+ average. He has always been a loner, and his only real human connections are with his immediate family, who live nearby. There is no prior history of psychiatric treatment. He strikes you as a rather shallow and empty man.

*Diagnostic Issues:* The history and evolution of his symptoms suggest the picture of acute psychosis (likely schizophrenia, although because of the absence of prior florid psychotic symptoms, initially this is best seen as schizophreniform disorder). He is evaluated medically to rule out disorders that may cause psychosis (none are found) and you learn that he takes no prescription medications. There have been no acute psychosocial stressors precipitating his slip into psychosis.

*Initial Medication Treatment Issues and Decisions:* The treatment of choice for schizophrenia is antipsychotics; Mr. P. is prescribed olanzapine 2.5 mg. b.i.d.

*Scenario One:* Mr. P. tolerates the olanzapine and on day 4 you increase the dose to 5 mg. b.i.d. Within a week he reports to you that he is sleeping better, and he appears somewhat less anxious. However, unrealistic thinking, auditory hallucinations and inadequate personal hygiene continue.

After 5 weeks of treatment, Mr. P. reports that the voices have stopped. Two weeks later, when again questioned about the buses, he states, "Oh, they aren't bothering me . . . I haven't paid much attention to them lately." Hygiene has improved a bit. He appears to be significantly less anxious, although he remains socially isolated and emotionally empty.

Treatment is continued for an additional ten months and then the olanzapine is gradually reduced over a period of six weeks. Mr. P. is stable and not psychotic. Follow-up appointments are scheduled on a once-a-month basis, and he is monitored closely, especially because his disorder is notoriously recurring.

*Scenario Two:* After two months of treatment with olanzapine, it is discovered that he has put on 7 pounds and has evidence of significant increases in triglycerides. The decision is made to switch the medication to aripiprazole which has a low incidence of metabolic side effects. This strategy proves to be effective in controlling the psychotic symptoms and normalization of his weight and lipid profile. He is showing a good response to the new medication, and continues to take aripiparazole for ten months. At that time you gradually reduce the dose.

In each scenario the clinician had the patient sign an informed consent for treatment and remained alert to the emergence of any abnormal movements that might signal the onset of tardive dyskinesia. Under the best of circumstances, Mr. P. will continue to be at risk for relapse, although since it was his first psychotic episode, it was reasonable to conduct a trial without medications about one year following his initial treatment. It is wise also to talk with the patient and (if appropriate) with his family about warning signs of possible relapse, so that should this occur, antipsychotic medications can be started immediately.

# Appendix A
# History and Personal Data Questionnaire

Date: _____

Name: _____ Date of birth: _____ Age: _____

Main reason for seeking help at this time: _____
_____
_____

## Current Problems or Symptoms

Please read each item below and determine which statement is true for you. Then, place an "X" in the appropriate box to indicate how often you feel the statement applies to you *during the past month or since your last visit.*

| EXAMPLE<br>Be sure to rate every item. | None or a little of the time | Some of the time | Most or all of the time |
|---|---|---|---|
| 1. I feel sad | | X | |

| DURING THE PAST MONTH OR SINCE LAST VISIT | None or a little of the time | Some of the time | Most or all of the time |
|---|---|---|---|
| **A** 1. Wake up at night in the early morning and unable to return to sleep | | | |
| 2. Very restless sleep; nightmares | | | |
| 3. Fatigue or loss of energy | | | |
| 4. Decreased sex drive | | | |
| 5. Unable to enjoy life; have lost interest in normal life activities | | | |
| 6. Have withdrawn from others | | | |
| 7. Strong thoughts about suicide | | | |
| 8. Loss of appetite | | | |
| 9. Memory problem, forgetfulness, poor concentration | | | |
| 10. Feel irritable or easily frustrated | | | |
| 11. Feelings of sadness or hopelessness | | | |
| 12. Sleeping a lot | | | |
| **B** 13. Decreased need for sleep | | | |
| 14. Increased sex drive | | | |
| 15. Increased energy | | | |
| 16. So happy or energetic that people describe me as "manic" | | | |
| **C** 17. Can't get to sleep | | | |

# Appendix A
## History and Personal Data Questionnaire, Cont'd.

| DURING THE PAST MONTH OR SINCE LAST VISIT | None or a little of the time | Some of the time | Most or all of the time |
|---|---|---|---|
| 18. Sudden episodes of nervousness or panic | | | |
| 19. Fear of losing self-control | | | |
| 20. Palpitations or rapid heart beat | | | |
| 21. Shortness of breath | | | |
| 22. Feel tense or anxious all day | | | |
| 23. Feel very anxious in social situations | | | |
| 24. Have recurring, troubling, thoughts, images or impulses that I can't get out of my mind | | | |
| 25. Repetitive behaviors such as excessive hand washing, etc. | | | |
| **D** 26. Feel very confused about my thoughts | | | |
| 27. Strange or bizarre thoughts | | | |
| 28. Hallucinations, hear voices, or see things that aren't there | | | |
| 29. Very peculiar experiences that others do not understand | | | |
| **E** 30. Feel ready to explode | | | |
| 31. Thoughts about harming someone | | | |
| 32. Excessive use of alcohol/drugs | | | |
| **F** 33. Unusual eating habits | | | |

| 34. Weight loss—How much in past month? | ____ lbs. |
| Weight gain—How much in past month? | ____ lbs. |
| Have you been trying to diet? | ____ Yes ____ No |

| 35. In the past I have tried to cut down on my use of alcohol or other drugs | ____ Yes ____ No |

### Previous Treatment for Psychological or Emotional Problems

| Year | Problem | Therapist/Location | Hospitalization or Medical Treatment |
|---|---|---|---|
| | | | |
| | | | |

### Do You Take Any of the Following Medications?
☐ Antihypertensives (for high blood pressure or migraine headaches)
☐ Steroids ☐ Hormones ☐ Tranquilizers ☐ Birth control pills

*Thank You*

# Appendix B
# Special Cautions when Taking
# MAO Inhibitors

*A Patient Hand-Out*

MAO Inhibitors can be very safe and effective antidepressant medications. However, certain foods and drugs must be avoided while taking MAO Inhibitors. Mixing MAO Inhibitors with the following drugs/foods can cause a serious rise in blood pressure.

## *FOODS TO AVOID*

- Cheese (Philadelphia cream cheese and cottage cheese are OK.)
- Chicken liver and beef liver
- Yeast preparations (Avoid Brewer's yeast, powdered and caked yeast as sold in health food stores; Bakery yeast is OK.)
- Fava or broad beans
- Herring (pickled or kippered)
- Beer, sherry, ale, red wine, liqueurs
- Canned figs
- Protein extracts (found in some dried soups, soup cubes, and commercial gravies)
- Certain meat products: bologna, salami, pepperoni, Spam

## *AVOID EXCESSIVE AMOUNTS OF THESE FOODS*

- Yogurt and/or sour cream
- Ripe avacados and guacamole
- Chocolate and/or caffeine
- White wine and liquors

## *MEDICATIONS TO AVOID*

- Stimulant drugs (amphetamines, dexadrine, benzedine, methedrine, methylphenidate)
- Diet pills
- Cocaine, "crack"
- Cold preparations, including over-the-counter products which contain decongestants (e.g., Sudafed, Contac, etc.). Antihistamines and aspirin are OK.

- Nasal sprays
- Adrenalin (Make sure that your dentist knows you are taking MAO Inhibitors because many local anesthetics contain adrenalin.)
- Please talk with your physician before taking any new medications (prescription or over-the-counter).

## SYMPTOMS OF DRUG FOOD INTERACTION

While taking MAO Inhibitors, if you ever experience the following symptoms, please contact your physician or an emergency room immediately.

- Severe headache
- Excessive perspiration
- Lightheadedness
- Vomiting
- Increased heart rate

*I have read and understand the above precautions.*

Patient's Name _____ Date _____
　　　　　　　　　　　　Signature

# Appendix C
## Caffeine Consumption Questionnaire

|  | Average number of ounces/doses/tablets per day | | Average total per day |
|---|---|---|---|
| ***Beverages*** | | | |
| Coffee (6 oz.) | 125 mg | × _____ | _____ |
| Espresso (1 oz.) | 35 mg | × _____ | _____ |
| Decaf Coffee (6 oz.) | 5 mg | × _____ | _____ |
| Tea (6 oz.) | 50 mg | × _____ | _____ |
| Green Tea (6 oz.) | 30 mg | × _____ | _____ |
| Hot cocoa (6 oz.) | 15 mg | × _____ | _____ |
| Caffeinated Soft Drinks (12 oz.) | 40–60 mg | × _____ | _____ |
| Energy drinks[1] (12 oz.) | 200 mg | × _____ | _____ |
| Chocolate candy bar | 20 mg | × _____ | _____ |
| ***Over-the-Counter Medications*** | | | |
| Anacin | 32 mg | × _____ | _____ |
| Appetite-control pills | 100–200 mg | × _____ | _____ |
| Dristan | 16 mg | × _____ | _____ |
| Excedrine | 65 mg | × _____ | _____ |
| Midol | 132 mg | × _____ | _____ |
| NoDoz | 100 mg | × _____ | _____ |
| Triaminicin | 30 mg | × _____ | _____ |
| Vanquish | 33 mg | × _____ | _____ |
| Vivarin | 200 mg | × _____ | _____ |
| ***Prescription Medications*** | | | |
| Cafergot | 100 mg | × _____ | _____ |
| Fiorinal | 40 mg | × _____ | _____ |

**TOTAL MG. CAFFEINE PER DAY**  _____  _____

---

[1]Energy drinks contain caffeine but also other stimulating herbs. Exact caffeine amounts are hard to determine, but most drinks have the effect of delivering an equivalence of 200 mg per 12 oz.

>250 milligrams per day *may* interfere with deep sleep

# Appendix D
## On-Line Practice Guidelines and Updates
## (Check for periodic updates)

American Psychiatric Association: PTSD, Bipolar Disorder, OCD, Alzheimers disease, Eating disorders, Major Depression, Panic Disorder, Schizophrenia
*http://www.psychiatryonline.com/pracGuide/pracGuideHome.aspx*

Texas Department of Mental Health: Texas Medication Algorithm Projects: Bipolar Disorder, Schizophrenia, Major Depression
*www.dshs.state.tx.us/mhprograms/TMAPover.shtm*

Sequenced Treatment Alternatives to Relieve Depression: STAR-D: National Institute of Mental Health
*www.nimh.nih.gov/health/trials/practical/stard/index.shtml*

Systematic Treatment Enhancement Program for Bipolar Disorder: National Institute of Mental Health
*www.nimh.nih.gov/health/trials/practical/step-bd/index.shtml*

Free Updates: Quick Reference to Psychotropic Medications: *www.Psyd-fx.com*

# References

American Psychiatric Association (2013) *Diagnostic and Statistical Manual of Mental Disorders: Fifth Edition (DSM-5)* American Psychiatric Publishing: Arlington, Virginia.

Clayton, A.H., et al. (2002) Prevalence of sexual dysfunction among newer antidepressants. *Journal of Clinical Psychiatry.* 63: 357–366.

Goldberg, Stephen (2011) *The Four-Minute Neurologic Exam,* MedMaster, Inc., Miami.

Goodwin, F.K. and Jamison, K.R. (2007) *Manic Depressive Illness: Bipolar Disorders and Recurrent Depression.* Oxford University Press: New York.

NIMH (2009) Sequenced Treatment Alternatives to Relieve Depression: www.edc.gsph.pitt.edu/stard.

Papakostas, G.I., Alpert, J.E., and Fava, M. (2003) "S-adenosylmethionine in depression: A comprehensive review of the literature." *Current Psychiatry Reports* 5:460–466.

*Practice Guideline for Major Depressive Disorder in Adults* (2003) American Psychiatric Association, Washington, D.C.: www.psych.org.

Preston, J.D., O'Neal, J.H., Talaga, M. & Moore, B.A. (2021). *Handbook of Clinical Psychopharmacology for Therapists* (Ninth Edition). New Harbinger: Oakland.

Roder, C., Schaefer, M., and Leucht, S. (2004) "Meta-analysis of effectiveness and tolerability of treatment of mild to moderate depression with St. John's Wort." *Fortschritte der Neurologie-Psychiatrie* 72:330–343.

Shea, S.C. (2006) *Improving Medication Adherence: How to Talk with Patients About Their Medications.* Lippincott, Williams and Wilkins: Philadelphia.

Texas Medication Algorithm Project: *http://asedillo.home.texas.net/tmap.htm*

# Index